SERVANT OF GOD

Sayings of a Self-Realised Sage

Swami Ramdas

SERVANT OF GOD

Sayings of a Self-Realised Sage Swami Ramdas

Compiled By

SUSUNAGA WEERAPERUMA

MOTILAL BANARSIDASS PUBLISHERS
PRIVATE LIMITED • DELHI

First Edition: Delhi, 1998

ISBN: 81-208-1328-6

MOTILAL BANARSIDASS
41 U.A. Bungalow Road, Jawahar Nagar, Delhi 110 007
8 Mahalaxmi Chamber, Warden Road, Mumbai 400 026
120 Royapettah High Road, Mylapore, Chennai 600 004
Sanas Plaza, Subhash Nagar, Pune 411 002
16 St. Mark's Road, Bangalore 560 001
8 Camac Street, Calcutta 700 017
Ashok Rajpath, Patna 800 004
Chowk, Varanasi 221 001

PRINTED IN INDIA
BY JAINENDRA PRAKASH JAIN AT SHRI JAINENDRA PRESS,
A-45 NARAINA INDUSTRIAL AREA, PHASE I, NEW DELHI 110 028
AND PUBLISHED BY NARENDRA PRAKASH JAIN FOR
MOTILAL BANARSIDASS PUBLISHERS PRIVATE LIMITED,
BUNGALOW ROAD, DELHI 110 007

Acknowledgements

Swami Satchidananda, the Managing Trustee of Anandashram, graciously granted me permission to quote extensively from the various publications of Anandashram. I am most grateful to him for his help, cooperation and advice.

The facts for *The Life of Swami Ramdas* have been taken from various books, notably *Passage to Divinity*: *The Early Life of Swami Ramdas* by Chandra Shekhar, which work incorporates the fine autobiographical essay by Swami Ramdas entitled *The Early Life.*

Vishwamata Krishnabai (Some Glimpses) by Swami Satchidananda is a very useful source of information on both Mataji Krishnabai and Swami Ramdas.

I thank Mr. V. Thanabalasingham for his extreme kindness in correcting and revising the manuscript.

I am very grateful to my wife Dr. Claudia Valentine Weeraperuma for the beautifully designed dust-cover of this book. Whereas the thorns represent the obstacles to God-realisation, the red rose depicts the Mystical Heart. The rose petals are symbolic of spiritual unfoldment.

Contents

Introduction

Swami Ramdas was not only an extraordinary spiritual master but also a master of the English language. He wrote with such style, precision and rare insight that his books are among the great classics of sacred literature. His elegant prose is replete with colourful metaphors and lovely phrases. In view of this fact, only phrases from his own works have been taken to form the chapter headings of this compilation.

The very *first word* of a chapter heading indicates what it mainly contains. Thus the subject of love predominates in the chapter entitled 'Love Breaks All Barriers'. The order of the chapters is determined by the *alphabetical sequence* of these first words. Therefore the CONTENTS list itself serves as a very useful subject index. This dictionary-like arrangement of the chosen excerpts dispenses with the need for a special subject index.

Glossary of Indian Terms

Amrita Vrishti (Amṛta Vṛṣṭi)	...	Shower of nectar
Ananda (Ānanda)	...	Divine bliss
Anandashram (Ānandāśrama)	...	Abode of bliss
Atman (Ātman)	...	Self
Avatar (Avatāra)	...	Incarnation of God
Bhagavad Gita (Bhagavad Gītā)	...	The Song Celestial of Sri Krishna, this being the dialogue between Sri Krishna and Arjuna on the battlefield of Kurukshetra
Bhagavan (Bhagavān)	...	Personal God of the devotee; form of addressing enlightened saints sages
Bhajan (Bhajana)	...	Religious music
Bhakta	...	Devotee of God
Bhakti	...	Devotion
Bhiksha (Bhikṣā)	...	Alms
Brahma	...	The Creator
Brahmacharya (Brahmacarya)	...	Spiritual discipline involving strict continence especially in regard to sexual activity
Brahman	...	The Absolute, Truth, Reality
Buddhi	...	Intellect

Darshan (Darśana)	...	Vision; sight of a holy person
Deva	...	Celestial being; a God
Dharma	...	Righteousness; the core of religion; that which upholds and elevates
Gerrua (Geruvā)	...	Ochre; the ochre cloth of a monk
Gita (Gītā)	...	*See* Bhagavad Gita
Gunas (Guṇas)	...	The three qualities—satva (harmony); rajas (activity) and tamas (torpor)
Guru	...	Spiritual teacher
Gurudev (Gurudeva)	...	Divine teacher
Gurukripa (Gurukṛpā)	...	The companion of the guru; the grace of the guru
Gurumantra	...	Holy formula given by the guru
Harijans (Harijanas)	...	The so-called untouchables; the children of God
Japa	...	The repetition of a mantra which is often a name of God
Jiva (Jīva)	...	Individual soul
Jivanmukta (Jīvanamukta)	...	A Self-realised person
Karma	...	Action
Karma Yoga	...	Yoga of selfless action; performance of one's own duty
Khaddar (Khaddara)	...	Hand-spun and hand-woven cloth from India
Lila (Līlā)	...	Play of the Divine
Loka Sangraha (Lokasaṅgraha)	...	Welfare of the world
Mahasamadhi (Mahāsamādhi)	...	The final merging into the Absolute with no return to corporeal existence
Mahatma (Mahātmā)	...	Great soul; sage
Mantra	...	A sacred formula, syllable or set of words of mystic import used in Japa

Maya (Māyā)	...	Illusive power
Nirguna (Nirguṇa)	...	Impersonal aspect of God
Nirguna Brahma (Nirguṇa Brahma)	...	Brahman without attributes; a term used to describe the Absolute
Nirvana (Nirvāṇa)	...	Liberation; absorption in the Absolute
Om	...	A sacred syllable
Prakriti (Prakṛti)	...	Nature; causal matter
Prem (Prema)	...	Divine love
Puja (Pūjā)	...	Worship
Puranas (Purāṇas)	...	Age-old stories of Hindu mythology
Rajasic (Rājasic)	...	Pertaining to Rajas, which is the quality of activity or restlessness
Ram (Rāma)	...	God's name; one of the ten avatars; form of address among sadhus
Ram Bhajan (Rāma Bhajana)	...	Devotional singing or meditation on God
Ram Mantram (Rāma Mantram)	...	The sacred formula with Ram's name
Ramnam (Rāmanāma)	...	Name of Ram; name of God
Sadhaka (Sādhaka)	...	Spiritual aspirant
Sadhana (Sādhanā)	...	Spiritual practice
Sadhu (Sāddhu)	...	Pious or holy person; sannyasi
Saguna (Saguṇa)	...	Personal God; God with attributes
Sagun Darshan (Saguṇa Darśana)	...	Vision of God with attributes
Samsara (Saṁsāra)	...	Worldly life or the wheel of birth and death
Sannyas (Sannyāsa)	...	Renunciation of worldly ties; the monastic order of life
Sannyasi / Sannyasin (Sannyāsī/Sannyāsin)	...	Monk; one who has renounced worldly ties for realising God
Sat-Chit-Anand (Sat-Cit-Ānanda)	...	Absolute Existence, Consciousness, Bliss

Satnam (Satnāma)	...	Eternal name
Satsang (Satsaṅga)	...	Association with the wise
Sattwic (Sāttvic)	...	Pertaining to Sattwa, which is the quality of harmony, purity, serenity
Sattva or Sattva Guna (Sattva/Sattva Guṇa)	...	The quality of harmony, purity, serenity
Shakti (Śakti)	...	God's power
Siddha	...	Realised person; a perfected being
Siddhis	...	Psychic powers
Sishya (Śiṣya)	...	Disciple
Sloka (Śloka)	...	Verse
Sri (Śrī)	...	A prefix meaning "sacred" or "holy"
Swarup (Svarūpa)	...	True Being; essential nature, form
Upadesh (Upadeśa)	...	Initiation or religious exhortation
Upasana (Upāsanā)	...	Worship
Vedanta (Vedānta)	...	The end of the Vedas; the Upanishads; the school of Hindu thought (based primarily on the Upanishads) upholding the doctrine of either pure non-dualism or conditional non-dualism
Vedantin (Vedāntin)	...	One who practises Vedantic philosophy
Vibhuti (Vibhūti)	...	A manifestation of Divine power
Vichara (Vicāra)	...	Inquiry into the nature of the Self
Vina (Vīṇā)	...	A stringed musical instrument from India
Yoga	...	Union of the jiva with God; method of God-realisation

The Life of Swami Ramdas

by

SUSUNAGA WEERAPERUMA

It was during my student days that I first came across the writings of an interesting Indian spiritual teacher called Swami Ramdas. Reading his articles in various periodicals became one of my favourite pastimes. His lucid explanations, devoid as they are of philosophical and rhetorical hocus-pocus, resulted in my gradually acquiring a new outlook on life, and his direct and devotional approach to the Absolute rekindled my flagging interest in religion.

Great was my joy when I heard in 1954 that the distinguished Swami was going to give some talks in Colombo (Sri Lanka) where I was studying at that time. Naturally I seized this golden opportunity of seeing him in the flesh and savouring the sight of his holy face. I was influenced by the Hindu belief that the darshan or the mere act of seeing a spiritual master and being in his presence is itself a blessing, regardless of whether one actually comprehends his message. Such a Darshan is regarded as a factor that furthers one's spiritual progress. Therefore I attended a crowded meeting in which Ramdas was going to speak. On this occasion I was accompanied by a friend who was an atheist. The tall bald-headed sage was seated on a dais. His upright and noble bearing bespoke confidence and inner peace. His large ears and prominent nose harmonised with his roundish face. Spotlessly dressed in white Indian clothes and clean-shaven, Ramdas radiated love and happiness from the very core of his being. I felt very comfortable and as it were bathed in the affection which emanated from him when I was in his presence. It was an emotion I shared with many of the others who were present. His all-embracing love endeared him to his disciples who affectionately addressed him as "Papa". He was wearing glasses, which subtly enhanced his venerable and professorial appearance. Sometimes he looked serious or solemn but whenever he smiled or laughed, which he frequently did, the eyes of Ramdas sparkled cheerfully and his face assumed an expression of innocence and childlike simplicity. Ramdas was surrounded by numerous disciples and admirers, who were gazing at him with awe. He spoke English so fluently that listening to him was a sheer pleasure. Occasionally he would crack a joke or tell an instructional anecdote. His talk was punctuated with many references to Ram (i.e. God). He assured the audience that God can be realised by the constant repetition of His name. My atheist friend became very restless and complained: "I can't continue listening to all this nonsense!"

I held his hand and whispered: "Please be patient! A God-realised man can't help talking about God, can he? Ramdas is true to his name because "Ram" means "God" and "das" stands for "servant". Servant of God—what an appropriate name!" My friend was so furious with me that he sighed with disgust and walked out of the lecture hall.

Revered as one of the greatest saints and spiritual teachers of modern times, Ramdas was born on April 10th 1884 in Hosdrug (Kerala, India). The boy was given the name Vittalrao.

The extraordinary lustre in his eyes was so striking that it was generally regarded as the most remarkable thing about Vittalrao. Such eyes often bespeak brightness of mind and in fact a wandering Sannyasin foretold a brilliant future for the boy. Concerning this rare light in his eyes, years later Ramdas modestly remarked: "This may mean anything or nothing."

His father, Balakrishnarao, began his career by working as a clerk for the government. Balakrishnarao's large family consisted of his wife and their thirteen children. Vittalrao, their sixth child, wrote appreciatively about his parents: "This divine couple, by their ideal life of householders, held up before the world an example as to how life in the world could be made supremely blessed and glorious. Selfless service at home and of the guests that poured into their house, was the keynote of their lives."

Vittalrao disliked the discipline of school life and "the so-called education of those days". His spirit yearned for freedom and adventure. Often he played truant. He not only distanced himself from school but also from arithmetic which was his pet aversion. He used to draw caricatures of his teachers in the classroom. From his teachers he received the most cruel chastisement although he loved them and his schoolmates. He was punished even at home. Full of pranks and mischief, he preferred climbing trees to attending school. How he enjoyed hopping from branch to branch in a monkey-like manner! How he amused himself by somersaulting continuously before a merchant who used to reward him with pieces of jaggery! His childhood was evidently an interesting blend of happy moments and trying experiences.

The religious atmosphere of his home was particularly suitable for the development of his soul—his grandfather's regular Puja, the singing of saints' songs by his grandmother, the devotions and prayers of his father, his mother's daily Japa and the reading of the Puranas by an aunt. Between the ages of six and ten he was drawn towards trees, solitary spots and vast spaces. Like Wordsworth he was a child of nature.

One of his favourite haunts was the old dilapidated fort of Hosdrug. The cool shade of the trees there and its silence was for him an elevating environment. Inside this fort was an ancient temple. He used to hover around this temple in a state of abstraction under the spell of nature's serenity.

During his childhood there was not in Vittalrao the least ambition for any worldly position or reward. It is significant that he already had the makings of a Sannyasin. He loved children and wished to remain one throughout his life. His favourite hobby was drawing pictures of persons and objects, which he was able to do because of an inborn talent for art. He also liked modelling with clay.

When Vittalrao was sent to Mangalore for his higher studies, although his indifference to school education still continued, there now grew in him a thirst for general knowledge, gained either from day to day experience or by reading books. He passed no examinations during the period of his primary and secondary education. He eschewed all games and scarcely mixed with the other boys, though his classmates and teachers had some affection for him. Neither did he read the textbooks nor attend classes regularly. He spent his time as a voracious reader of books from his school library. He developed a liking for English literature and read the works of the great masters with the result that quite early in life he achieved a high degree of proficiency in English.

He was a good conversationalist and a raconteur with a fine sense of humour. Even in later life he would raise roars of laughter in his listeners through his keen sense of the comic. What appealed to him was not the serious side of life but the lighter. He was however by no means a superficial person. Another conspicuous early trait of his was a spirit of independence which enabled him to have his own distinct outlook on life. Both during his childhood and during his youth he did not care much what clothes he wore or how he wore them. He was so unconventional that he became indifferent to his external appearance. Throughout his life he remained extremely simple in his tastes and attitudes.

Vittalrao next joined the Christian High School at Udipi. It is hardly surprising that he failed the matriculation examination; thereafter he returned home where, in his own words, he "enlisted himself to the sublime profession of idleness!" For a time he immersed himself in the activities of the Amateur Drama Society in which he played a prominent part. Vittalrao played a minor part in Shakespeare's *King John*; later when he played the role of a clown in another play he brought down the house; finally, in a drama dealing with the life of Shivaji he acted the part of Samarth Ramdas, the great Maharashtrian saint and guru of Shivaji.

The time spent in school was not altogether wasted because it enabled him to become intimately acquainted with the Bible. He made the following observation about his own religious evolution: "The old Bible of the Christians, and the ancient religion of the Hindus in several parts of it, depicted God as a God of retribution, who cursed those who acted contrary to His commands. Ramdas knew the power of the Bhakti cult of the Hindus and the teachings of Buddha and Christ. All these presented before us a God who is compassion, kindness and forgiveness. To trust Him means to be entitled to His grace, and this Grace frees us from all hate, anger and lust and converts us into His likeness. Ramdas had now begun to understand clearly the meaning and purpose of human life. This great ideal of God as love fired his heart and was slowly influencing his life."

In his writings, as in the above-mentioned quotation, Swami Ramdas refers to himself as "Ramdas" instead of "I". He always speaks of himself in the third person. On many occasions he has mentioned that Ram and Ramdas are actually one because he has realised his oneness with Ram.

Vittalrao's parents sent him to the Madras Arts School where he studied drawing and engraving. As he was fond of art he progressed remarkably well there. Afterwards he went to Bombay where he studied textile manufacturing in the Victoria Jubilee Technical Institute. His reminiscences of this period are interesting: "God's ways are inscrutable. The subject in which he had great interest and for which he had great love was given up and he had come to Bombay to study another subject for which he had absolutely no liking. Still three years were spent, not with the object of gaining any pass or distinction in the Institute training, but in studying life in close grips, studying men with intimate touch and association, reading books from libraries which could provide any and every kind of book on any and every conceivable subject. He saw life in its highest heights and in its lowest depths."

During the first two years of his stay in Bombay, Vittalrao lived with his best friend, Vadiraj, an employee in a German dye firm. Vadiraj looked after him with tender loving care. Vittalrao reciprocated his friend's love with the same ardour. Theirs was a platonic relationship. Vittalrao has stated "Ramdas has seen brother loving brother, mother loving her sons, and friend loving a friend, but the love which this friend bore for Ramdas was something very rare. It can be compared to all the love of these three persons and much more. There was not a day when he returned from his office without a great longing to see Ramdas....Whenever he got anything for himself , he would also get the same for Ramdas."

Vittalrao has also left us a moving description of his beloved friend's demise and how this loss caused him much sadness: "...the friend who was all love and kindness to him and under whose loving care and affection Ramdas spent his years in Bombay, had a severe attack of typhoid. His mother, two wives and some other friends were in his house at the time. When his condition began to deteriorate, he did not wish that any of his relations should go to his room except Ramdas and the doctor. Medicines and food were given to him by Ramdas as he would not accept them from the hands of others. Ramdas used to be with him almost the whole day. He stopped going to the Institute during these days. Till then Ramdas had not been near any person at the last stage when life was going out of the body. Ramdas did not leave the friend's bedside and he saw how gradually the disease was gaining the upper hand and wringing out his life....When death claimed the friend, Ramdas' heart was agitated with great sorrow. He started crying like a child which had lost its mother. In fact, some years later he lost his mother, but the pain of that loss was not as severe as this....The impression which this sad event left on him deepened his indifferent attitude towards the high aims and ambitions of this transitory earthly life. When circumstances force the soul to turn to its immortal, changeless existence, full of light, peace and joy, it gets now and again glimpses of this supreme state, just as one gets flashes of light from the sun for a brief period whenever the clouds that cover it pass on." This heart-rending experience was an important landmark in the path leading towards his eventual spiritual Liberation: it turned his attention from the ephemeral to the eternal.

It was through his friend Vadiraj that he gained access to a library containing the great treasures of English literature. He continued reading widely, beginning with historical works and then changing over to poetry. Some of the poets whom he greatly admired were Shakespeare, Goldsmith, Byron, Browning, Cowper, Wordsworth, Shelley, Southey, Tennyson and Keats. Next, he read the works of Burke, Carlyle, Ruskin, Schopenhauer and Emerson. He read them with great avidity but "could not find any suitable principles on which life could be safely founded though they did provoke thought and kindle an enquiry after Truth". One senses a certain disappointment in Vittalrao: it was not mere intellectual stimulation that he was seeking but something else—a sound philosophy of life perhaps—which he had so far failed to find in books. It was then that he discovered the publications of the Rationalists' Press Association of America. After reading the works of Ernst Haeckel, Grant Allen and others "the faith created and nourished during his childhood vanished at a sweep, and he turned into a sceptic. He felt that whatever he had read or heard from the scriptures about God and His worship, belonged to mental hallucinations. God was merely an idea conceived in the human brain. In reality there was no God; Nature alone caused all movements, and the two had no relationship or connection with each other. Ramdas remembers the expression often used in this regard— "a fortuitous concourse of atoms". Everything happens by chance and there is no such thing as an immanent and overruling power that guides the destinies of all things. The scientific manner in which the Rationalists sought to prove that God did not exist, dashed his faith in God to pieces....It is no doubt easy to slip from faith in God to atheism; the path being downward and slippery, the time taken for the change is short and quick". He continued his reading, which included the Greek philosophers, Roman orators, German and French dramatists, American and English humorists and books on crime and detection.

His religious faith had almost disappeared but it revived when he came across the works of Swami Vivekananda, Ramakrishna Paramahamsa and Swami Rama Tirtha. This renewed faith took deep root in him but in a different form because the ceremonial and ritualistic aspects of religion no longer appealed to him. "His ideal was a spiritual life built upon a sure and pure foundation of a strictly moral life and action. The idea of caste and creed vanished from his mind. He believed in a God who is the father of all members of the human race. God is universal, the divine source of all that exists. His heart bent before such a God." From now onwards he concentrated on the Hindu and Christian scriptures and when he read a translation of the *Bhagavad Gita* it was for him a spellbinding experience.

All this extensive reading was at the expense of his studies at the Institute! Although he had been treating his studies with indifference, he managed to pass the final examination by studying intensely for a month or two prior to it. Thereupon Vittalrao obtained his diploma in textile manufacture.

Vittalrao was resolutely against marriage when a matrimonial proposal was first made to him. But in 1908 at the age of twenty-four, after some hesitation, he married Rukmabai, a cultured and religious lady, because he did not want to displease his parents who had arranged the union, especially his sick and bedridden mother. He viewed the institution of marriage from a spiritual standpoint: "Marriage is considered to be a sacrament. It is to bring about the union of two souls so that they can walk hand in hand, as it were, on the path that leads to Divinity. But this significance is nowadays completely absent in the alliance of the two persons brought about by the ceremony or ritual of wedlock. In Ramdas' case the marriage was not a success as he fully expected it. But that life gave him an experience which was needed for the complete understanding of life and its implications. Just as the harmonious mingling of two souls provides us with opportunities to realise the beauty of life, so also the constant friction between two souls removes all the dross that covers the soul so that it may appear in all its nakedness before the Great Being from whom it has manifested."

Vittalrao now entered an unsettled phase in his life. His chequered career consisted of short periods of employment which were interspersed with longer periods when he was out of work. When his elder brother started a handloom and soap-making business in Madras, Vittalrao helped him a great deal, although his training in textile manufacture was more appropriate for a power-driven cotton mill. For a short time he secured employment as a spinning master in a cotton mill at Gulbarga. He lost this job when the management of the mill changed hands.

It is an interesting fact that adverse circumstances did not depress him; on the contrary, he tended to become more optimistic. Life is full of challenges and he was willing to accept them cheerfully. He regarded the movement of life as a huge joke: whatever happened, favourable or unfavourable, he gladly accepted it, seeing it as the Lila of the Lord. This attitude prevailed throughout his life, even prior to his spiritual metamorphosis, which will be described later in this account.

Wherever he worked, Vittalrao was appreciated by his superiors, subordinates and colleagues for he was efficient and painstaking. He also desired to help the less privileged workers.

Once when Vittalrao was holding the position of spinning master in a mill at Gadag, a certain disciplinary action that he took against a worker resulted in some of them wanting to assault him as he left the mill in the evening. Although some of the assistants warned him of their violent intentions, he ignored these warnings, and walked towards the gate where he confronted a group of workers who were armed with sticks. He simply smiled and remained unruffled and they did not attack him!

Next he worked in a mill at Quilon, where he was later promoted to the position of manager. The mill was in dire financial straits. There he was badly off for he did not get the full salary that was his due. He was so hard-pressed for money that he had to close down his own house and send his wife back to Mangalore. One Sunday when Vittalrao was alone in his office, a fitter who had not received his wages for several months, stood at the entrance to his office with a large knife and threatened that unless his wages were given immediately he would not allow Vittalrao to leave the place. Vittalrao not only told the desperate man that he was prepared to fight his way out but he also brandished a heavy rosewood ruler. This attitude quite surprised the fitter who, noticing Vittalrao's grim determination, fled in fear. Vitalrao was a brave person who did not mind facing dangers and risking his own life.

Five years after Vittalrao's half-hearted marriage his daughter Ramabai was born. His professional career, like his domestic life, was not without troubles and he was sometimes out of work. When he was employed at a waste mill in Madras for a period of two years the mill's proprietor cheated Vittalrao, who was deprived of more than half his salary. Whenever Vittalrao pressed for his money, the dishonest proprietor would say "Brother, God will give; God will give" but the Almighty failed to provide it! Next he got a job as a spinning master in the Coimbatore Spinning Mills whither he moved with his wife and child. The European managers of the mill became displeased when he championed the cause of his subordinates, especially that of the mill-hands. During this period the death of his beloved mother was an event that affected him very deeply. He had to rush to Hosdrug for the funeral. When he returned to Coimbatore he was asked to quit his job. He was again in search of employment, soon after the emotional crisis caused by the loss of someone so near and dear.

On one occasion Vittalrao found work in a mill owned by an irascible old man who was given to using violent and abusive language. None of his employees escaped his verbal attacks. Vittalrao's contract was only for a period of four months. When Vittalrao warned his boss that his violent words would not be tolerated even for a moment, within two months of his commencing work the proprietor paid his full salary for the stipulated term and dismissed him. This incident illustrates Vittalrao's daring and his sturdy independence.

At a time when he was filled with disgust because of the need to look for employment every now and again, he received an invitation from his father-in-law at Mangalore to join him in his cloth business. The offer was accepted towards the end of 1917. Their commercial partnership foundered before long because Vittalrao disliked the chicanery and subterfuge usually associated with trade.

Inside a room he started dyeing and printing Saris. When his wife was critically ill with a severe attack of smallpox, Vittalrao knelt before a photo of Sri Pandurangashram Swamiji of Chitrapur Math, Shirali and prayed for her recovery. Tears rolled down his cheeks as he prayed and he experienced a certain peacefulness of mind. From that moment the patient's condition began to improve and she was soon back to normal. This experience resulted in an important change in Vittalrao. He became increasingly religious and would talk only of God and the teachings of the saints. He would also pour out his heart, especially to his elder brother Sitaramrao who was also devotionally inclined. His business expanded and flourished and the two brothers cooperated to establish the firm Sri Sitaram Vittal Co. Later their brother Narsingrao also joined the enterprise as a partner. The goods produced by this company were highly appreciated and even won a gold medal at an exhibition. But the business seemed doomed to disaster: the wages paid to his workmen were too high; members of staff received frequent increments; the profits were cancelled out by the overheads; there was no capital to back up the firm nor reserves to draw on in times of financial hardship. Vittalrao was generous to a fault and he lacked the calculating shrewdness that is characteristic of many a successful businessman.

Adversity was his constant companion. Not only was his business deteriorating but his wife had become a chronic asthmatic. Such misfortunes were counterbalanced by the joy of caring for his only child. He loved his daughter with all his heart, taking her to school in the mornings and bringing her back in the afternoons, playing games with her and answering all her questions. But before long this love for his only offspring was going to be superseded by his universal vision—his own child and all other children would be viewed with the same all-embracing love, unblemished by any feeling of partiality or discrimination whatsoever.

He spent an hour every evening at the house of his brother Sitaramrao with whose children he would participate in the communal singing of hymns before an image of Sri Krishna. During the Bhajan he would experience a state of ecstasy. He also began studying anew the teachings of Sri Ramakrishna, Swami Vivekananda, Swami Rama Tirtha and other classics such as *Yoga Vasishtha*. These pursuits quickened his spiritual evolution.

This was the time when Vittalrao began the spiritual practice of frequently repeating 'RAM'—the sacred name of the Lord. It was a Sadhana that brought him much peace and happiness.

His business was faring so badly that creditors were insisting on the settlement of their dues. Only a miracle could save him from financial ruin. Then, providentially a prosperous lawyer turned up at Vittalrao's house and offered to be his business partner. This person had recently given up his practice at the Bar in response to Mahatma Gandhi's call to boycott the courts. Such was Vittalrao's honesty that he did not withhold any information from him concerning the penurious state of the company's affairs. The lawyer not only became a partner in the firm but also liquidated all its debts and even invested a large sum of money in new machinery for the production of Khaddar.

At a time when fortune was at last beginning to smile on his business enterprise, Vittalrao did not cash in on his luck to become rich or accumulate capital as indeed many a normal entrepreneur would have done. Instead his mind was turning increasingly towards the Supreme Being whose name he kept on repeating continuously, even during the greater part of the night. He gave up taking his night meal and his lifestyle became austere. Neither his alarmed wife nor his daughter succeeded in dissuading him from following this new course of life. He strongly felt that it was God who had chosen this particular path for him.

An important stage in his spiritual growth was reached when he received spiritual initiation from his own father. How Vittalrao's unshakeable trust in Ram sustained him during this time is best described in his *In Quest of God*:

> "For nearly a year, Ramdas struggled on in a world full of cares, anxieties and pains. It was a period of terrible stress and restlessness—all of his own making. In this utterly helpless condition, full of misery, "Where is relief? Where is rest?" was the heart's cry of Ramdas. The cry was heard, and from the Great Void came the voice "Despair not! Trust Me and thou shalt be free!"—and this was the voice of Ram. These encouraging words of Ram proved like a plank thrown towards a man struggling for very life in the stormy waves of a raging sea. The great assurance soothed the aching heart of

helpless Ramdas, like gentle rain on thirsting earth. Thenceforward, a part of the time that was formerly totally devoted to worldly affairs was taken up for the meditation of Ram who, for that period, gave him real peace and relief. Gradually, love for Ram—the Giver of peace—increased. The more Ramdas meditated on and uttered His name the greater the relief and joy he felt. Nights, which are free from worldly duties were, in course of time, utilised for Rambhajan with scarcely one or two hours' rest. His devotion for Ram progressed by leaps and bounds."

"During the day, when cares and anxieties were besetting him due to monetary and other troubles, Ram was coming to his aid in unexpected ways. So, whenever free from worldly duties—be the period ever so small—he would meditate on Ram and utter His name. Walking in the streets he would be uttering, "Ram, Ram". Ramdas was now losing attraction for the objects of the world. Sleep, except for one or two hours in the night, was given up for the sake of Ram. Fineries in clothes and dress were replaced by coarse Khaddar. Bed was substituted by a bare mat. Food, first, two meals were reduced to one meal a day and after sometime this too was given up for plantains and boiled potatoes—chillies and salt were totally eschewed. No taste but for Ram; meditation of Ram continued apace. It encroached upon the hours of the day and the so-called worldly duties."

"At this stage one day, Ramdas' father came to him, sent by Ram, and calling him aside, gave him the Upadesh of Ram Mantram—"Sri Ram, Jai Ram, Jai Jai Ram!" assuring him that if he repeated this Mantram at all times, Ram would give him eternal happiness. This initiation from the father—who has thereafter been looked upon by Ramdas as *Gurudev*—hastened on the aspirant in his spiritual progress. Off and on he was prompted by Ram to read the teachings of Sri Krishna—"The Bhagavad Gita," Buddha—"Light of Asia," Jesus Christ—"New Testament", Mahatma Gandhi—"Young India" and "Ethical Religion". The young plant of Bhakti in Ram was thus nurtured in the electric atmosphere created by the influence of these great men on the mind of humble Ramdas. It was at this time that it slowly dawned upon his mind that Ram was the only Reality and all else was false. Whilst desires for the enjoyment of worldly things were fast falling off, the consideration of *me* and *mine* was also wearing out. The sense of possession and relationship was vanishing. All thought, all mind, all heart, all soul was concentrated on Ram, Ram covering up and absorbing everything."

From time immemorial men and women from the Indian subcontinent and elsewhere have forsaken their worldly possessions to find God or Truth. They have endured tremendous hardships and privations in the course of their spiritual quest. Of the countless thousands who renounced the world only a few like the Buddha, Mahavira and Ramana Maharshi in modern times were conspicuously successful but many never seemed to accomplish anything. It was towards this well-trodden spiritual path that Vittalrao was moving.

He was becoming more and more ascetical. Dressed simply in a Dhoti and a collarless shirt as well as a white cap, he happily walked the streets, constantly repeating the sweet and sacred Mantra OM SRI RAM JAI RAM JAI JAI RAM. (Interestingly enough, Ramdas had prefixed "OM" to the Mantra given to him by his father. Ramdas was much attached to Swami Ram Tirtha whose Mantra was OM—the primary or original sound from God).

Outwardly he was thin and pale but inside he was in a state of ecstasy on account of this ceaseless chanting . After rising at four o'clock in the morning he would have a bath and thereafter meditate until about seven. Such was his austerity that he ate only when he experienced pangs of hunger. Anxious relations of Vittalrao, who were naturally concerned about his well-being, tried to dissuade him from a life of self-mortification but he remained adamant.

Steeped though he was in religious devotion, this zealousness was certainly not at the expense of his daily duties for he conscientiously attended to his work at the weaving establishment. Devotion to the Deity had the effect of softening his heart, so he treated his workmen kindly and regarded his subordinates as his equals. He felt great compassion for those in pain. When, for instance, he once saw a carter mercilessly beating the bullocks he begged the man not to strike these poor dumb animals but his words were ignored. Vittalrao had to run away from the scene for he could not bear to see such cruelty. He advised his wife and daughter never to injure or cause any harm to any creature.

He was vaguely conscious that the time was fast drawing nigh when he would renounce everything but he did not know how or exactly when this would happen. He was eagerly awaiting the severance of all his earthly ties and his subsequent merging with the Divine.

The factors that induced Vittalrao to renounce the world and dedicate himself to Ram have been described in his *In Quest of God*:

> "So, one night while engaged in drinking in the sweetness of His name, Ramdas was made to think in the following strain:
>
> O Ram, when Thy slave finds Thee at once so powerful and so loving, and that he who trusts Thee can be sure of true peace and happiness, why should he not throw himself entirely on Thy mercy, which can only be possible by giving up everything he called 'mine'? Thou art all in all to Thy slave. Thou art the sole

> Protector in the world. Men are deluded when they declare, 'I do this, I do that. This is mine—That is mine'. All, O Ram, is Thine, and all things are dône by Thee alone. Thy slave's one prayer to Thee is to take him under Thy complete guidance and remove his 'I'-ness.

This prayer was heard. Ramdas' heart heaved a deep sigh—a hazy desire to renounce all and wander over the earth in the garb of a mendicant—in quest of Ram wafted over his mind. Now Ram prompted him to open at random the book—"Light of Asia" which was before him at the time. His eyes rested upon the pages wherein is described the great renunciation of Buddha, who says:

> "For now the hour is come when I should quit
> This golden prison, where my heart lives caged,
> To find the Truth; which henceforth I will seek,
> For all men's sake, until the truth be found."

Then Ramdas similarly opened the "New Testament" and lighted upon the following definite words of Jesus Christ:

> "And everyone that hath forsaken houses or brethren, or sisters, or father or mother or wife or children or lands for my name's sake, shall receive a hundredfold and shall inherit everlasting life."

Then again he was actuated in the same way to refer to the "Bhagavad Gita"—and he read the following Sloka:

> "Abandoning all duties come to Me alone for shelter, sorrow not, I will liberate thee from all sins."

Ram had thus spoken out through the words of these three great Avatars—Buddha, Christ and Krishna—and all of them pointed to the same path—renunciation. At once Ramdas made up his mind to give up for the sake of Ram, all that he till then hugged to his bosom as his own, and leave the Samsaric world. During this period, he was very simple in his dress which consisted of a piece of cloth covering the upper part of the body and another wound round the lower part. Next day, he got two clothes of this kind dyed in Gerrua or red ochre, and the same night wrote two letters—one to his wife whom Ram had made him look upon for sometime past as his sister—and another to a kind friend whom Ram had brought in touch with Ramdas for his deliverance from debts. The resolution was made. At five o'clock in the morning he bade farewell to a world for which he had lost all attraction and in which he could find nothing to call his own. The body, the mind, the soul—all were laid at the feet of Ram—that Eternal Being, full of love and full of mercy."

He wrote his wife a touching letter in which there are references to 'Rame' which is the pet name of his daughter Ramabai:

Dear Sister,
You are to me only a sister in future. Sri Ram, at whose feet I have surrendered myself entirely has called me away from the past sphere of life. I go forth a beggar into the wide world chanting the sweet Name of Sri Ram. You know I have no ambition in life except to struggle for the attainment of Sri Ram's Grace and love. To that aim alone I dedicate the rest of my life and suffer for it—suffer to any extent. We may not meet again—at least as husband and wife. Walk always in the path of God and truth, and make Rame do the same.

Don't give up the spinning-wheel. It will give you peace and happiness. Let Rame also work it.

Sri Ram's blessings on you and Rame. He protects you both.

Yours affectionately

27-12-22 —P. Vittalrao

On December 27th 1922 whilst still a young man of 38 he severed all his worldly ties and became a religious mendicant, turning his back on the comforts of hearth and home and preferring instead the humility and insecurity of a homeless life.

After bathing in the sacred Kaveri River at Srirangam, he cast his white clothes into the waters as an offering and wore the simple orange-coloured clothes of a renunciant. Next, he prayed to Ram:

> "O Ram! O Love Infinite—Protector of all the worlds! It is by Thy wish alone that Thy humble slave has been induced to adopt Sannyas. In Thy name alone, O Ram, he has given up Samsara, and cut asunder all bonds, all ties."
>
> "O Ram, bless Thy poor devotee with Thy grace. May Ramdas be endued with strength, courage and faith to carry out in Thy name, Ram, the following vows and bear all trials and all kinds of privations that may beset the path of a Sannyasi in his passage through the rough and perilous life of a mendicant:
>
> 1. This life be henceforth entirely consecrated to meditation and the service of Sri Ram.
> 2. Strict celibacy be observed, looking upon all women as mothers.
> 3. The body be maintained and fed upon the food procured by Bhiksha or on what was offered as alms."

From now onwards Vittalrao is called Ramdas or "Servant of God": it is a singularly appropriate name for it marks his spiritual rebirth.

This inner regeneration filled him with extreme happiness. Freed of the past with all its problems and sorrows, Ramdas described the consequent state of bliss in these words: "The thrills of a new birth, a new life, filled with the sweet love of Ram, were felt. A peace came upon the struggling soul of

Ramdas. The turmoil ceased. Ram's own hands seemed to have touched the head of his slave—Ram blessed. O tears, flow on, for the mere joy of deliverance! Sorrow, anxiety and care—all vanished, never to return. Glory be to Ram!"

In 1923 Ramdas had the privilege of seeing Ramana Maharshi and being in personal contact with this great saint for about five minutes. This memorable meeting proved to be a turning point in the life of Ramdas as he himself gratefully acknowledged in his *The Divine Life*:

> "Ramdas thinks it will not be inappropriate to recall here his own experiences....at Tiruvannamalai, and to describe how, by having Darshan of Sri Ramana Maharshi, he was prepared for the Universal Vision he had a few days afterwards on the sacred Arunachala Hill. It came about in this way. Soon after Ramdas had the Sagun Darshan of God in the form of Sri Krishna, he left Mangalore, as prompted by the Lord, and went about wandering from place to place. In the course of these wanderings, God in His own mysterious way took Ramdas to Tiruvannamalai. Ramdas' condition those days was like that of a child, waiting always for the mother's guidance. He had absolutely no Sankalpas or plans of any sort. So when a Tamilian Sadhu asked Ramdas to accompany him to Tiruvannamalai, Ramdas readily obeyed and simply followed the Sadhu. The latter took him to Sri Ramana Maharshi. The very sight of the Maharshi left an indelible impression on Ramdas. Ramana Maharshi stands for Nirguna Brahman and Universal Vision. So he poured into Ramdas, the necessary power and grace to obtain this vision."
>
> "When Sri Ramana intently gazed on Ramdas and the eyes of both met, Ramdas felt He was pouring into him His spiritual power and grace in abundance, so much so that Ramdas was thrilled, as His divine light shone on his mind, heart and soul. Sri Ramana's eyes

always radiated a splendour, which was simply unique and irresistible—a splendour mingled with infinite tenderness, compassion and mercy. The few minutes that Ramdas spent in His holy company meant a momentous impetus in his spiritual career."

"After obtaining Maharshi's Darshan, Ramdas went up the Arunachala Hill and remained there in a cave. During his stay in the cave, Ramdas was chanting Ram-Mantra day and night. He had absolutely no sleep and for food he used to take only a small quantity of boiled rice, which he himself prepared out of the alms he got. After twenty days' stay in the cave, in the above manner, one morning Ramdas' eyes were filled with a strange dazzling light and he realized the Presence of the Divine everywhere. This new vision of the Universal gave him such waves of ecstatic Bliss that he started running about here and there on the hill, embracing trees and rocks, shouting in joy 'This is my Ram, this is my Ram!' He could not resist the rising ecstasy. This was his first experience of Universal Vision."

As a wandering mendicant Ramdas went to all parts of India. He had a large number of followers who were fascinated by his life and teachings. Posterity is indebted to him because he has fortunately left detailed descriptions of his travels and experiences, which have been published as two books entitled *In Quest of God* and *In the Vision of God.*

A feeling of triumphant ecstasy pervades much of the poetry of Ramdas:

O Ram, I see Thy form on every side;
In all the worlds Thy light and glory abide.
O Ram, Thou art the sun that shines on high;
Thou art the moon and stars that deck the sky.

O Ram, Thou art the life that fills all space,
And sets the whirling universe in its race.

O Ram, I see in hills Thy form divine,
In waters vast that flow and wave and shine.

O Ram, I see Thy light in jungles wild,
In trees and plants and verdure mild.
O Ram, all life reflects Thy godly light,
Thou art all in all—Love, Bliss and Might.

—OM—

Is there any connoisseur of devotional literature who would not like to savour the poetry of Ramdas and find spiritual sustenance therein? *Poems* by Ramdas consists of the bulk of his poems which were composed at different times for *The Vision*, an international monthly dedicated to "Universal Love and Service", which was founded by Ramdas in October 1933 and personally edited by him during the first two years. In a letter to a Western devotee he stated that "Ramdas' spiritual experiences have reached such a stage that he can hardly give expression to them. However in the poems in *The Vision* from month to month, he is struggling to give utterance to them." His lyrical lines are the sweet outpourings of a heart that is inseparably linked to the Divine.

From the far corners of the globe people flocked to the feet of Ramdas, seeking his fatherly advice on the problems of life in general and spiritual matters in particular. Many also chose to correspond with Ramdas and his written answers to questions have been published in 2 volumes entitled *Letters of Swami Ramdas*. He certainly had the gift of lucid exposition. An extract from a letter written in 1928 illustrates the kind of spiritual guidance he provided: "Ours is to remain ever in complete surrender to Him. He does everything for our best. No condition is miserable for us, if we put full faith in this truth. Kings and potentates are unhappy in spite of their wealth and external glory, because of their lack of faith in the beneficent providence of God. The Almighty Lord of the worlds seated in our hearts is the sole doer. We are mere puppets. Let Him make us dance as He wills. Ours is not to question why. Difficulties and worries are not due to outside causes. They are due to a mind not surrendered up to God."

The world tour that was undertaken by Ramdas, lasting from August 1954 until January 1955, was one of the highlights of his later years. All his speeches and talks during these travels, including his answers to questions, were first published in 10 volumes by Anandashram. The following extract is from a famous speech by Ramdas delivered in Bombay on the eve of his departure to Europe:

> "It was thirty years ago that Ramdas was first taken up by God and made to do everything as He willed. From that time onwards, Ramdas has been going round India, propagating the message of love and peace to all people who come in contact with him. But now it is His will that Ramdas should go outside India and move about in the world so that he can meet more of His manifestations in order that he may see in them also the same Beloved One he sees here, and has been seeing all along during his tours in different parts of India."

"Now, the object of his going to foreign countries, as willed by the Divine—Ramdas uses the word 'foreign' as it is a common usage, but in fact there is nothing foreign to him as the whole world is his home—is to propagate the ideal of Universal Love and Service. Ramdas can spread this message only in one way; and that is by beholding his Beloved in all, so that his love may flow out and inundate the entire world, removing all man-made distinctions and enabling us all to stand united as one world family. It is one Truth that pervades everywhere and all humanity is the expression of that Truth. Ramdas is going abroad to show all how it is possible to achieve this exalted experience. Every one must realise that the Divine is within him."

Papa's foremost disciple was Mother Krishnabai who first came into contact with him in 1928. At that time she was eagerly searching for a Guru. The shocking news of her husband's sudden death, leaving her and her two sons behind, filled this poor widow with sorrow. It was a major crisis in her life. She was deeply affected by the thought that she could not be present at her husband's bedside during his last moments. Her spiritual progress was so rapid that in 1930 Mother Krishnabai realised her oneness with the Absolute. Thereafter she dedicated her entire life to the service of Papa and his mission. She played a very important role in the founding of the Anandashram at Kanhangad, which was inaugurated on May 15th 1931. When she accompanied Papa in his world tour in 1954 many friends and devotees felt they had been blessed by the experience of meeting them personally. After Papa's Mahasamadhi she guided the affairs of the Ashram and ministered to Papa's worldwide spiritual family until her own Mahasamadhi on February 12th 1989.

Mother Krishnabai's autobiography entitled *Guru's Grace* describes her ordeals and years of struggle as well as her meeting with Papa, which culminated in her realisation of the Supreme. This book was rendered into English by Papa himself from the Kannada. It was his last literary legacy to the world. Papa paid many tributes to her remarkable qualities in his *Introduction* to this work. "Krishnabai's life presents", he wrote, "a practical illustration of how an individual can live a life of spontaneous and intense activity while ever fixed in the Divine Consciousness born of complete self-surrender." This autobiography is unusual in that it is addressed entirely to Papa and all the persons mentioned in it are regarded as Papa himself in different forms.

The following passage from the autobiography is representative of the spirit of surrender and devotion that is characteristic of this book: "O love-incarnate Papa! Wherever we went, thousands of people used to come to you for Darshan. As their hearts were filled with great love and devotion for you, the moment they had your Darshan their hairs would stand on end and tears of joy would flow down their eyes. Some devotees, finding you in their homes, were so transported with joy that they forgot their bodies and sat still without knowing what to do."

Papa's numerous discourses and conversations as well as his pithy and sparkling answers to questions in India and elsewhere were faithfully recorded by Swami Satchidananda. These have been published in several volumes, notably *Ramdas Speaks, Ramdas' Talks* and *The Gospel of Swami Ramdas.* These invaluable books are a source of inspiration to spiritual aspirants. Swami Satchidananda was very intimately associated with Papa from 1947 to 1963. For a time he served Papa as his secretary. He also looked after him with loving care: massaging Papa's body, applying medicated oil on his head and legs, giving him insulin injections (Papa was a diabetic and a rheumatic), shaving him and even preparing Roti (home-made wheat bread) for Papa. A man who selflessly dedicated his life to Papa, the Swami is today the Managing Trustee of Anandashram.

It was Papa's 80th year. On the evening of July 25th 1963 he had a severe heart attack. He felt a choking sensation. He was collapsing but his two closest disciples, Mother Krishnabai and Swami Satchidananda, managed to take him to his cot. While lying down there, he would suddenly sit up, chanting "Hari, Hari, Hare Ram". With the name of God on his lips Papa breathed his last. With all his mind and heart Papa had adored the sheer sound of the Divine name and it is significant that he even chanted it when he was sinking fast. The devotees were stunned and heartbroken by the suddenness of the end.

Placed on a perfumed bed of fragrant flowers, Papa's body lay in state. Those present were quick to notice that the saint's face had a certain serene and sublime radiance. Friends and devotees poured in and offered flowers, sandalwood and incense. People gathered to pay their last homage to a great soul. Two days later his mortal remains were consigned to the sacred fire and cremated whilst hundreds of mourners chanted Ramnam.

Adoration of the Lord

The greatest acquisition of human life is Divine love. Divine love is the love for the Lord seated in the hearts of all beings and creatures. This love is attained by the devotee in the first place only through the realization of the Lord in his own heart. The Lord is the master of the worlds. He pervades the entire universe. He is the supreme ruler of all the planes and spheres of existence. Since He is everywhere and all, to behold Him in all beings and love them all, is the true adoration of the Lord. In this vision of love, the apparent good and evil have no significance. This love is based upon equality and a consciousness of universality. Divine love is absolutely pure and crystalline. It does not see distinctions, and so has no likes and dislikes. It flows from the heart of the devotee, and floods the world embracing and absorbing all alike, just as the light from the sun shines equally on all. It sheds its sweetness on all to the same degree. The devotee who has realised this exalted love is spontaneously blissful in all his activities, since these are permeated through and through with love! The real joy of the eternal is conceived in the womb of Divine love. Divine love expresses itself in cheerfulness, contentment, self-sacrifice, forgiveness, compassion and peace.

This love is absent in that heart in which, in the place of the supreme Lord, ego has installed himself. The ego is the cause of soul's bondage and misery. The moment the soul realises his supreme and divine nature by union with the Lord in his heart, he becomes the very lustrous moon emitting always soft and soothing rays of Divine love. The ego obstructs the free flow of the Divine life in the human being. So to earn the supreme blessings of this glorious love, a one-pointed devotion to and adoration of the Lord of the universe is the way, the means and also the goal.

Adoration of the Lord signifies a loving remembrance of Him at all times, and this remembrance can be most easily effected by taking constantly the Lord's Divine Name.

The Divine Life, pp. 138-139

Avatars Release a World-Redeeming Spiritual Force

A question is raised whether an Avatar and a God-realised soul possess the same power and vision and carry out the same mission in this world. Surely, so far as the knowledge of God is concerned, both are on the same plane, but in the field of action the Avatar brings down the light and power of the supreme Truth to a greater mass of humanity than a God-realised soul does. The Avatar embodies not only the inner perfection of the Spirit but also exercises all the power and glory of the Divine: whereas a God-realised soul throws the light and power upon a smaller portion of humanity and works under certain limitations. It is rightly said that the God-realised soul can be compared to a well and an Avatar to a river in flood: while the former can satisfy the thirst of a few who seek the well, the swollen river spreads out its water all over the country allaying the thirst of innumerable beings and creatures. So in the spiritual awakening of humanity the work of an Avatar is decidedly more extensive and far-reaching than that of a God-realised soul.

Moreover there is a clear assertion made by the Avatar that he has descended on the earth with the special mission of liberating mankind from ignorance and bondage. A God-realised soul does not make such a declaration. We see that the great Avatars like Krishna, Christ, Buddha, Mohammed and Zoroaster are saviours of humanity and redeemers of all fallen souls.

Again if we study their teachings, we find Avatars have a message for the whole world. They preach universal love as the highest attainment which alone can establish unity, harmony and brotherhood in the world.

Some people would have us believe that the Avatars never existed and that their lives have only an allegorical meaning and relate the inner transformation of a soul from ignorance to higher divine nature. This opinion also is not true. All the Avatars, after whom the principal religions of the world are founded, are historical personages. Their historicity is denied because it is hard for some people to accept that God who is infinite and impersonal could manifest Himself within the limitations which the assumption of a physical body imposes upon Him. God, who is all in all, is at once limited and unlimited, finite and infinite, personal as well as impersonal. Encased in relative and perishable bodies as Avatars, God has through them exhibited omnipotent powers. They have done miraculous things which, judged by the unalterable laws of Nature, are impossible. Some may doubt whether the miracles did happen at all. They even go to the length of opining that they are sheer concoctions. This view cannot carry much weight with those faithful devotees who, after a sufficient advance on the spiritual path, have experienced the wonders of the inner life. They know that in the realm of the Spirit nothing is impossible. In the light of the writer's unique realisations, he can boldly declare that a person inspired by the spirit of God can reveal miraculous powers. Apart from the power of performing miracles which Avatars possess, they release a world-redeeming spiritual force by which they transform men steeped in ignorance and sin into veritable angels of purity, wisdom, love and peace. Whoever comes in contact with them even in thought and meditation becomes illumined by their light and power. Avatar is God Himself in human form.

The Divine Life, pp. 152-154

Beauty in the Eyes of God

Question: *There is a Japanese theory that flowers and plants have a wish to contribute to external beauty. If we cut off a branch or pluck flowers with the idea of making the plant perfectly beautiful, then it joins in the happiness.*

Ramdas: Nothing of the kind. That is beauty in the eyes of man. There is a beauty of nature, that is, beauty in the eyes of God, only when the plants are left as they are. The plants have been given certain branches and certain directions of growth according to the will of God who is the source of all beauty. Everything is beautiful in His eyes. What is beautiful for Him may not be beautiful for the human eye because man's sense of beauty is different, and therefore he cuts and shapes them as he likes, only to cater to his own ideas of beauty. We must see as God sees. Then only we shall appreciate beauty as it is. The sense of beauty differs with different people. That is not the real sense of beauty which is God's, according to which He has created this universe.

Question: *There is a problem for the gardener. He loves the plants very much but he has to prune them sometimes very drastically, cutting almost everything down because when the plants are cut that way, they will grow quickly.*

Ramdas: It is not so much for beauty that he cuts them. If they are cut, they may give better and bigger flowers.

Ramdas Speaks, vol. 2, p. 37

Bhakti is the Adoration of God

Bhakti is an intense longing and love for God which enables the aspirant to keep up a constant remembrance of Him, thus purifying his emotions and elevating his thought to the consciousness of the Reality. Bhakti is the adoration of God, who dwells in his own heart and fills the universe, and surrender of all his actions to Him. Here a fit of renunciation seizes him—a mental recoil from the unrealities of life that had so long enthralled him. Through the exercise of an awakened intellect he now begins to discriminate the real from the unreal—the eternal from the non-eternal.

The Divine Life, p. 114

Bhakti means making God the supreme ideal of life. For the Bhakta there is no other thought but of Him, and no other ambition but to attain Him. His mind runs towards God through a ceaseless flow of remembrance. The Bhakta's heart is ever agitated with the waves of hope and aspiration for the vision of God. His restless nature, besides urging him to dwell constantly in the thought of God, directs his steps to the feet of saints and drives him from place to place on visit to noted shrines. As the child away from its mother is stricken with anguish and sorrow for the sight of her, so the Bhakta insistently weeps with the longing for the Darshan of God. He finds life dry and tasteless until he meets his supreme Beloved. The more he meditates and contemplates upon the great attributes of God, the more he begins to feel his own littleness and unworthiness, and prays to his Beloved to elevate, enlighten and purify him, so as to make him fit to be accepted as His child and servant.

For the Bhakta, God is the very embodiment of love, compassion, forgiveness and grace. He visualises his God in the recesses of his own heart. He surrenders completely in thought, word and deed to his Beloved, and adores Him with an unflinching devotion. By a constant meditation of the Lord, the Bhakta imbibes into his own being the Divine attributes, ultimately reaching a status of perfect union and oneness with Him. Compassion, mercy and love now illumine the nature and therefore all actions of the Bhakta. He becomes the very image of God, for the impurities and weaknesses having been removed by the grace of the Lord, he stands revealed as the very sun of Truth, radiating all around him the rays of love, kindness and peace.

Now the greatest virtue that shines forth in all its splendour in the Bhakta is forgiveness. As God has forgiven him, so he forgives all in the world who wrong or have wronged him. He ever returns good for evil, both in thought and action. He is self-sacrificing to a degree. He is ever willing to serve and toil for others, to give them solace and relief. He loves all with an equal vision, be he friend or foe, rich or poor, good or wicked, high or low, wise or ignorant. He endures peacefully ignominy and persecution and gives himself away in every manner for the good of others. He is ever contented, ever pure and ever cheerful. He is unassuming and humble in all he does. He recognises God as all in all. He experiences God seated in his heart as causing, by His power, all movements in the world. He beholds and feels God's presence everywhere. Verily, he always lives and moves in God and is the very being of God.

The Divine Life, pp. 120-121

Bhakti is the adoration of the supreme Lord of the universe beyond everything else in the world. This one-pointed adoration makes the devotee keep his mind ever engaged in the remembrance and contemplation of the Lord. The Divine idea seizes the mind of the devotee to such an extent that the most attractive objects of life cease to fascinate him. He talks, laughs and often weeps in his madness for the Lord. As he progresses on the path of devotion he is weaned away from the petty and transient pleasures of the senses and remains, as it were, dead to them. His one passion is to see God, know God, and be entirely merged in God.

The Divine Life, p. 122

Bliss of the Atman

Everyone who is in the grip of struggle for the attainment of the eternal values of life knows that life's fulfilment and its ultimate fruition depends upon the immortal bliss and peace of the Atman. He further knows that this unchanging Truth can be his, only when the mind is withdrawn from the external attractions of the world, only when he has conceived a revulsion of feeling towards the pleasures of the senses, only when the false cravings of his soul for the unstable and ephemeral things of life have ceased and disappeared. These are the necessary conditions for the realisation of the immortal peace and joy of the Atman.

The Sages have declared: There is no higher gain in this existence than the bliss of the Atman. When you have once found it, you are utterly free from the clutches of mental turmoil and the fetters of death and misery. Suppose a man has come by a perennial spring of nectar at which he can quaff to his heart's content and thus satisfy the thirst that parches his soul, would he hanker after the unwholesome water of dirty ponds that brings disease and consequent pain and misery?

If you would really enjoy the blessings of a true and independent life, then by a concentrated and sustained effort seek the bliss of the eternal. Nothing else in this world can quench the flames of desire that rise and burn in your heart. Liberation is spoken of as the realisation of the immortal Divinity dwelling within you. Be intoxicated with the joy that never changes, that ever exists. Joy, bliss and peace are your quest. Independence and freedom are your goal.

If you have understood, by ransacking the depths of your desire-ridden heart, the true purpose of your life, you will surely have discovered that nothing short of the attainment of an immortal state would completely satisfy the innate aspiration of your soul: The passing glamours of life, the gilded pleasures that you pursue, are the will-o'-the-wisps that delude the mind and throw you into the prison of ignorance and death. Therefore, seek the eternal, seek that which never dies, never changes—that which is your real spirit, the one deathless truth of your being. Do not be deceived. Wake up from the sleep of ignorance. Be aware of your eternal Self. Tear up the veil between you and your God, and know that you and He are one. Declare with all the joy that you can command: "I am the all-pervading, indestructible, beginningless and endless Truth, whose nature is perfect peace and bliss. I am the self-existent, all-powerful Reality. I am the free, ageless, birthless, everlasting Spirit. Disease, poverty, fear and want have nothing to do with me. I am bliss—pure bliss: peace—pure peace. I am the Light of lights. I am the primeval source of all things. I am God and there is none but 'I'." Meditate thus until you are inebriated with the thought of your Divine state, until you merge and lose yourself in the limitless ocean of your immortal existence and make this blessed human life abundantly blessed.

The Divine Life, pp. 70-71

The Buddha: Truth is Inexpressible

Buddha is a veritable sun of spiritual effulgence. He came into the world more than 2500 years ago and his power and glory still hold sway on a large portion of the human race. He is a redeemer and saviour of souls, just as Krishna and Christ are. His burning renunciation, his absolute purity in thought, word and deed, his heart throbbing with love and compassion towards all living creatures in the world, his illuminating presence that brings solace and peace to sufferers caught in the grip of pain and misery, stand out in bold relief whenever we meditate upon him.

The message of non-violence and love which issued forth from his divine lips so long a time ago still reverberates and will reverberate throughout the passage of time. It is a message which brings solace to the aching heart of humanity. There is no period in the history of the world when this great message is more needed than at the present time. The world has been and is in the throes of discontent, discord and distress, and Buddha's exhortation of love and peace can alone relieve the earth from its heavily pressing burden of ill will, hate and injustice and the consequent agony of disaster and war. Buddha's teachings, taken in their totality, can be resolved into one illuminating short edict, namely, "Give love for hate." This brief sentence is pregnant with the greatest uplifting and divinizing power, and when it is followed with faith and surrender, it can transmute the life of a human being into one of supreme tranquillity, light and beneficence.

Buddha never sought to define the ultimate Truth which all beings are in quest of, because Truth is inexpressible. It is realised only by purifying our mind, emotions and actions; and for achieving this end he sets down certain rules of conduct which, if adopted, will lead the soul to a state of deliverance from the deep-seated ignorance with which it is enveloped. This deliverance of emancipation, Buddha calls Nirvana. Nirvana is the attainment of supreme inner freedom and peace in which the soul is freed from the thirst for sense objects and the enjoyments accrued from them. He teaches that by the negation or elimination of that which is transitory or unreal, the ineffable Reality can be realised. He emphasises that absolute purity is the only sure way to Nirvana. Compassion towards all beings is both the means and result of such a realisation.

Let us therefore learn from this great World-Teacher the lesson by following which we can make our lives in every way blessed, a great force for radiating love, light and peace towards all our fellow-beings on this earth. It is by love we find union with them. It is by love that we conquer our lower nature, baser instincts and desires. It is by love that we ignite within us the flame of true wisdom and knowledge. It is love that makes our hands and feet engage themselves in service, without expectation of any reward, for healing the sorrows of the world. Buddha is a very embodiment of this love. May his love awaken the hearts of all beings, inspiring them to live together in perfect harmony and goodwill and establish thereby a lasting spirit of unity and brotherhood on this earth!

The Divine Life, pp. 175-176

Communion with Your Eternal Beloved

What is there sweeter in the world than to hold communion with your Eternal Beloved? He is your never-failing companion and friend. He resides in the inner chamber of your heart and is also present everywhere about you. He is the soul of your soul, the life of your life. In the absolute sense, you and He are one.

If this love of intimate comradeship with your Beloved does not inspire your life, even if you have all other things, your life is lived in vain. See your Beloved in the face of all beings and creatures. Verily, He has become the whole universe. Wherever you turn, there He is. The bliss of His presence is inexpressible. Why run away from Him and seek to attain peace in aloofness? Allow your life to mingle with His life, that is the universal life. He is a calm, serene, changeless Spirit and, at the same time, He is a world player. He dances in the hearts of all beings and creatures. He is at once wisdom, power and love.

How beautiful are the images in which He appears! He is the essence of all grandeur and majesty. He is the smile on the face of the innocent child and the power that sits on the brow of the king. He is the love that bubbles in the heart of the saint. He is the radiance that shines upon the whole creation. Who can describe His greatness? Why talk of Him in terms of abstract philosophy, while He is the very nectar which you can drink and enjoy? He permeates your physical frame and tingles in every atom of it.

You are wise, you are well-read and you have gone through spiritual practices; you have put on the garb of sanctity, you can preach and you can pose—these are all nothing if you do not experience the blissful union with the Beloved. You can meet Him in the streets, in the bazaar, on the hills, in the cottages of the poor, in the palaces of kings, in hermitages and jungles, in workshops and offices—at all places. He is with you. How sweet, how charming is His constant company! Why do you miss Him? Be humble. Reduce yourself to the very dust of His feet. But dwell in Him and be enchanted by His company. Lay aside your pride. What are you worth if you do not have Him? You may sit on an eminence but without Him you cannot be happy. You may own millions but without His smile beaming on your face you are poor indeed. Enrich your life by His light, love and joy. How sweet and great He is!

Seek the Beloved. Feel His presence. He is thy own Self. Have Him at any cost. Find Him and enjoy eternal felicity. That is why you are here.

The Divine Life, pp. 22-23

Compassion is the Noblest Virtue

Compassion is the noblest virtue that adorns the heart of a human being. Real peace and contentment can reside only in that heart which feels for the sufferings of others. The heart does not stop at being merely touched by the woes of its fellow beings, but it overflows in acts of kindness and love. The heart that feels but does not express itself in selfless action is like a spring dried up at its very source.

O friend, if you would have freedom from fear and sorrow, and enjoy the supreme blessing of everlasting peace, expand freely your heart so that it might go out in waves of compassion to soothe and alleviate the distress of the world. Whenever a kindly feeling rises in you, let not selfish thoughts stifle it. If you would realise the endless bliss of immortality which alone is your real quest—although you are unaware of it—liberate the heart from its hardness by the magic touch of compassion.

Life is a short span and the pleasures you derive in it are transient and fleeting. In pursuing these shadows, you are heading towards darkness and are becoming oblivious of the exalted and ever-blissful Truth which is your real being. Through the infusion of compassion and love let your heart be illumined and purified so that you can behold yourself as all the world. A narrowed and cramped heart is the cause of misery and pain. Your liberation lies in your hands. God who dwells in you ever awaits to succour you. Seek His aid and fight with the enemies—lust, greed and wrath—by the weapons of His grace and power. Do not forget the Divine Master. He is all compassion and mercy. Feel His presence in you and everywhere about you—in all beings and creatures. Install Him in your heart as the very embodiment of love. Compassion will then be a natural quality of your heart. The softened heart will then melt away in the sweetness of your immortal life, and all your actions will give out the veritable fragrance of kindness and love. Now your selfless life will always yield peace and joy to yourself, and offer relief and delight to all in the world.

The Divine Life, pp. 105-106

Contemplation of God

The mind which constantly contemplates upon God, imbibes into its being His immortality, love and joy. The saying: "As a man thinketh, so he becometh," is eminently true. The individuality conceived of by the mind as a stable and real existence, must, by means of meditation, merge in the universality of God's existence. It is the experience of every aspirant on the spiritual path that the more he devotes the mind to the exalted thought of God, the more he is absolved from its impurities.

The principle is: take in brilliant and elevating ideas, and automatically the low and grovelling thoughts will be purged off. Just as the application of soap removes the dirt of the cloth turning it clean and white, or just as light dispels darkness and illumines space, so also a sustained recollection of God, destroying all the distempers of the mind, purifies and ennobles life. It is rightly said that one should not unnecessarily exert oneself for subduing the mind, but what one has to do is to dwell in the contemplation of God, and by this method not only purify the heart but also simultaneously fill it with the light, love and joy of God.

Verily, there is no peace for man until his mind is liberated from the clutches of passion, until the wisdom of the Eternal enlightens him.

Therefore, raise your heart, mind, soul and body to the throne of the almighty Lord within you in concentrated adoration and worship. Let the harassing complexity of life be substituted by harmonious simplicity. So regulate your life as to attain to a vision which enables you to be naturally friendly towards all creatures and beings in the world. Let humility be your shield, love your weapon, and a blissful life of service the aim and mark. Don't be satisfied with anything less than the universalisation of your outlook upon life. This is the Atma Darshan sung of by the sages of yore. It is a supreme state in which the notion of the body, the sense of apparent diversity and the erroneous consciousness of the ego have no place. It is the vision of the pure, resplendent spirit that pervades all beings in the universe. It is a vision of yourself as the indwelling Reality in the all forms and existences. It is a vision of indescribable ecstasy born of the knowledge of one eternal substratum or Soul that fills and overflows to infinity the world phenomena.

How do you reach the summit of this transcendental Reality?—by recollection, contemplation and meditation. Give your thought entirely to God and you are bound to realise that you are God Himself. Before the glory of this attainment, all other aspirations of man are flat and childish. When you can tune your mind with the all-powerful Master of the universe and realise deathless peace, liberation and bliss, is it worth while for you to pursue the ephemeral prizes and achievements of the world, however great and glossy they might seem? What a tremendous privilege this human birth is! Human life can have the full value set on it only when it is utilised for achieving the loftiest purpose for which it is meant.

Hence, turn your mind, day by day, towards the immortal source of your life—God. Let your life be more and more filled with Divine effulgence and love. Let your actions flow like a gentle stream singing the melodious song of Divine service. Be gifted with the sight of the sage, and behold your Beloved everywhere—aye, your Beloved everywhere.

The Divine Life, pp. 72-73

Death is False

My thought flies like a bird carrying the message of peace to all the worlds. A light goes out of my eyes that illuminates the entire cosmos. My heart responds to the rhythm of a heavenly music that resounds through all space.

The angels hover round me—the Devas of the other worlds—the embodiments of the omnipresent Spirit. They look human, but they are my God in so many forms. The Deva, man, bird and beast are all the varied shapes taken by my God. They are all sweet and good.

I see Him and am lost in Him. I hear Him and am attuned with Him. I touch Him and become one with Him. In all planes of life I am united with Him.

With outstretched arms He beckons me and I rush to Him, and I am caught in His ecstatic embrace. I shut my eyes in the intoxication of joy. 'O Beloved!'—that is all I could say. O my Lord, my God, my supreme Mother, I am eternally Thine—I am Thyself.

How strange! I am Thyself, yet I am Thine. When I sit silent with eyes closed, I behold all the worlds and beyond in me, and myself in all the worlds and beyond. Whenever I am before anybody, I look at him as myself. His movements are mine. When he talks and acts, it is all myself.

Death is false. Every particle of the body in all its states is ever intensely alive—dust or ashes. Soul, body, universe, all beings and things are all one. Matter is Spirit, Spirit is matter. All is He and His expression!

Spirit is still, but it sings sweetly and universes are born. They live in the infinite ocean of the Spirit like ice floating on water.

All minds and all bodies! You are dear to me. You are made of my substance. My substance is omnipresent, immutable Spirit. Still, there are ripples in me. They are the planets, stars and stellar spheres, ever in motion, whirling through the glowing etheric atmosphere. All hail, all hail to Thee!—the one Truth—the one Reality.

The Divine Life, pp. 54-55

Divine Consciousness Destroys the Ego-Sense

To conquer the lower nature and reveal the glory of the Divine is the purpose of Sadhana. The Sadhaka, before he starts on this enterprise, is a mere tool in the hands of the ego which dominates and controls him in every way. To destroy the ego-sense is not an easy task. A supreme endeavour backed up by divine grace is necessary. The mind has to be brought into subjection and all the desires vanquished. So the Sadhaka's life is a life of tremendous struggle.

The Sadhaka should, in the first place, be fired with an intense aspiration for his spiritual regeneration and the attainment of the highest goal—God. Then, contact of saints should follow. The ego, having its sway on him, refuses to yield and sets up all kinds of obstacles on his path. It often poses as the Supreme Himself and leads him astray. At the beginning the Sadhaka finds it hard to distinguish the divine guidance from the promptings of the mere mind. The method, by adopting which he can safely progress on the divine path, is to surrender himself entirely to the all-powerful God within him by constantly thinking of Him and His attributes. It is by constant remembrance of Him alone that he develops the needed soul-force to put down the mind and its machinations and rise superior to it. Instead of being the slave of the mind, he should be the master of it.

As the Sadhaka gets more and more into communion with the Divine, the power of the ego diminishes until the ego itself disappears when the full blaze of God-realisation floods his being. It must not be forgotten that, for the Sadhaka, to realise God is to assert his own immortal and divine Self. Just as light dispels darkness, so the divine consciousness destroys the ego-sense. The mind-stuff, which was all along the cause of ignorance and the resultant chaos, should totally cease to exist. It is now that God's mastery in the human vehicle is evident in all its sublimity. Such a Sadhaka has become one with the supreme Reality and his external life becomes a spontaneous outflow of divine energy, radiance and joy. He becomes the very embodiment of divine Love. The struggle has now ended and victory achieved—a victory over all that is undivine in him—a victory that brings him a state of perfect freedom and bliss.

Whenever violent passions seek to subdue the Sadhaka and cause a sense of frustration and despair in him, he should sit in a prayerful attitude, calm and silent, and take complete refuge in God to escape the blast. Detachment from the mind and constant watchfulness over it is the way to gain control over it. Detachment can be possible only when the heart is attuned with the eternal Self. Heroic spirit and readiness to endure pain, and grit to face failures and defeats, having full confidence in the ultimate success of his quest, should be the qualities of a true Sadhaka. He should cling to God with all his strength, with all his heart and with all his soul. In fact the Sadhaka's triumph is God's own triumph.

The question is asked why God at one stroke does not lift the Sadhaka to the realm of spiritual freedom and peace. He, as an ignorant human being, is a delicate and weak instrument. Before the fullness of the divine illumination can be revealed into it, it has to be, by a steady process, strengthened and made fit in all respects for the great consummation. God's power works in the Sadhaka, who has resigned himself to Him, for a gradual divinisation of every part of his being. The antagonistic influences are now replaced by the suzerainty and all-controlling power of God. In short, God alone rules supreme in him and absorbs him into His resplendent Being. Now the Sadhaka and God are one and the aim of human life is fulfilled.

The Divine Life, pp. 27-28

Divine Consciousness of the Eternal and Cosmic Reality

Divine consciousness is the consciousness of the eternal and cosmic Reality. It is attained by transcending the human or individual consciousness. It is born of the soul's complete union and absorption in the all-pervading Oversoul. Here the ego notion which binds the soul to a narrow vision is totally absent giving place to an extensive and unlimited vision in which all the visible and invisible worlds are included and absorbed. The individual sense has absolutely no place in this exalted state. The person who has reached this spiritual height, though appearing to possess an individual sense is, in truth, entirely free from it. He lives, moves and acts from the standpoint of the universal and super-universal Reality. He realises the truth that there is only one existence and one power both as the unmanifest and manifest Reality. He feels at all times that he is one with all beings, creatures and things in the world both physically and spiritually. He knows that all movements, changes and activities going on in him and everywhere about him are of one single cosmic power.

What is the nature of actions performed by a person who has attained this supreme state? The same power that activates all things in the universe, is also responsible for the actions of the persons who have attained divine consciousness. The manifestation that we behold before us is a concrete expression of the divine Shakti. The person of knowledge knows this truth whereas the ignorant one is unaware of it. The knowledge of it enables the former to become not merely a vehicle of the divine power, but also the very embodiment of it. So it is evident that actions are possible in this state. The action performed by one who has realised the Truth, is a spontaneous outflow from the divine source. Hence even in a life of great activity, the God-realised soul enjoys the bliss of immortality, for the dynamic nature that reveals itself in action is the manifest aspect of the underlying, silent and cosmic Spirit.

Even after reaching this great height of the all-comprehensive vision of the Reality in which all diversity is dissolved, the God-realised soul assumes a position separate from the great Truth. He calls himself the son, child, servant or devotee of God. Here the duality is assumed, knowing that the devotee and God are truly one. Why this assumption? Because, in the sphere of activity the God-realised one prefers to play the part of a lover or servant in order to enjoy the ineffable bliss of love. Love works only on the plane of duality. All his actions, great or small, bear the stamp of love, for love is his being and love is his life, and in love he finds the fulfilment of his existence.

Based upon the realisation of his oneness and identity with the supreme Spirit, the devotee still plays the part of a servant or child and acts in all manner of ways as the very incarnation of God. His touch or sight redeems the fallen soul—brings light and happiness where there is darkness and sorrow. He is the real saviour of mankind.

The Divine Life, pp. 18-19

The Divine is the One and Only Reality

Ignorance or delusion, i.e., Maya, sets us on the belief that this body of ours is real and makes us forget the all-pervading Divine being who is the one and only reality. Living in this ignorance, our sole outlook on life becomes one continued service of this inconstant, unreal and perishable body. Our concern then is always to find ways and means as to how best to nourish and protect this body. What best food should be given to it? What clothing should this body wear? What ornaments should adorn it? What must be put on the head, what on the feet, what must be used to cover the legs, what to dress the body with, and what rings, what bangles, what necklaces, what jewellery should it be decked with? These are the things in which we engage ourselves. The body demands fine and luxurious food to eat, rich clothing to wear, a soft bed to lie upon and brilliant ornaments to adorn itself with. It calls for fine music for the ears, sensuous sights for the eyes, sweet aroma for the nose. O! the delusion of this body! We fidget about the whole day and night in pursuit of the requirements of this transient body. It wants a spacious, decorated, well-furnished house to live in. It wants so many things and beings to satisfy its momentary pleasures. We are every minute engaged in this mad rush of satisfying the cravings of the body; and the mind and the senses are in their full play, making havoc of our lives. In our blind pursuit we hate and get angry with our brethren, and snatch ruthlessly from them, and secure for ourselves, what our mind has set itself upon, as our want. After all, to what purpose? For a momentary gain, for a passing happiness. In this struggle, what do we experience? Misery, pain, disappointment, anxiety, care, disease and ultimate destruction.

The all-loving, all blissful Reality—Ram—is entirely forgotten. We forget the fact that we come alone, naked into the world, and leave it at the end in the same condition. The hoarded wealth, the loved relations, the cherished fame, the vast property, the gold we value so much, all, all we leave behind, and carry with us only a load of sin which we gather in the course of our strife and struggle to amass these worldly baubles. O! vain life, O! vain world, how attractive are thy wiles! The Maya is such—ignorance is such! Instead of being the servant of the all-powerful, ever-existing and all-loving Ram, we become slaves of our bodies, senses and the mind. O Ram, how wonderful is the illusion in which Thou keepest us all! By Thy grace alone, can we free ourselves from it. O Ram, have pity on us and liberate us and take us on to your holy feet.

The world is simply a vanishing play of the three Gunas—Satwa, Rajas and Tamas. All forms are merely the result of the Gunas. Therefore, we should never associate ourselves with these Gunas and the appearances caused by them. But who has assumed these forms and the Gunas that are Mayavic or illusive? It is the one supreme, imperishable Being, the only Reality. Therefore, let the forms and Gunas produce on us no impression whatsoever, except that of merely reminding us of the Reality that appears to us as these forms controlled by the Gunas. Diversity is false. Unity or oneness is Truth. Let our mind be always fixed on Truth—the only Truth. Let the mind be never allowed to dwell upon objects or forms. Let the mind be not engaged in judging or criticising things and forms. In order to stop the wandering of the mind that runs away to think upon various objects which as different entities are all unreal and therefore disturbing, we must develop the practice of immediately associating the thought of the Reality with the thought of the object, whatever it may be. If you go on having this practice, the diversity gets merged into the real unity. Maya gets absorbed in the Brahman. The turmoil of the mind is gone, and, in its place, settle down, the everlasting peace and bliss, because the Reality itself denotes, and is, peace and bliss.

At the Feet of God, pp. 43-45

Divine Protection and Grace Through Unshakable Faith

When an earnest aspirant or devotee is on the path of God-realisation, he meets with innumerable obstructions and difficulties, but God's mercy is so great that the adventurous soul is endowed by Him with the necessary strength and will to endure or overcome them. The mysterious manner in which the benevolent Master of the worlds guides and protects him is simply wonderful. If we examine the earlier life of intense struggle of an aspirant for self-control and attainment of the Divine, in every case, we find that the Lord did, with infinite love and kindness, watch over and protect him. In fact, the opposing or resisting forces on the path seem to be a part of God's own plan so that the aspirant by contending against them may develop the needed will-power for the subdual of the mind and its restless nature.

The moment the devotee takes refuge in God, acknowledging Him as his all in all, the moment his entire being is surrendered up to Him, the moment all his life's activities are completely dedicated to Him, the feeling or consciousness of peace, security and freedom which he attains is verily inexpressible. Then the devotee is ever free and blissful like a child under the benign care of the Divine Mother.

What is required is a fixed faith and a steady aspiration or hunger for God. Thereafter the progress or evolution towards the vision of God becomes easy, for at every step, even when he has to conquer the worst enemies within the mind or the greatest obstacles outside, he feels that the hands of the Divine are ever holding him, infusing into him courage and enthusiasm.

Every saint, who has achieved the highest spiritual experience, lays before you that during the period of his Sadhana, God himself saved him from many a pitfall and dangerous situation in inscrutable ways. He bears witness to the fact that God is all powerful and His compassion and love for His devotees is unlimited. He tells you emphatically: put yourself in the hands of God and you are safe.

Life's fulfilment and the revealment of its glory, power and victory lie in its perfect dedication to God. Man has to rise beyond himself, transcend all the lower conceptions of his nature, subdue the false impulses of the mind and conquer the vitiating influences of the ego and thus rising superior to them all, meet his supreme Beloved in his own heart and in the hearts of all objects in the world.

The Divine assurance, "My devotee perisheth never", is a promise of the utmost significance. Really, there is none who is so full of kindness and love as our eternal Mother, none so forgiving, none so tender, none so benevolent as She. Realising this let everyone entitle himself or herself to Her Divine protection and grace, through unshakable faith and entire self-surrender. Merge yourself, therefore, in Her resplendent being, and attain to a life imbued with the consciousness of immortality, peace and bliss.

The Divine Life, pp. 69-70

Divinity Permeates Everything

No renunciation but understanding of the source from which all have come forth is the answer to the life problem. Human or animal outlook is false. Dispel separation or illusion; all thoughts and feelings then function as before, but infused with the light of the Divine.

The Divine alone exists. There is none other than the Divine. To be aware of this is true knowledge, and not to be aware is gross ignorance. While the latter creates a sense of separation and diversity, the former makes for a consciousness of unity and oneness. The first Is Truth, the second untruth.

To wear beads on the body, to besmear ashes on the forehead, or to dress in coloured clothes, mean nothing. The hallucination that you are separate from your fellow being must go. In and as the supreme Spirit, all are one. Live always in this your natural consciousness. Then you are really happy and free.

Rend the veil of illusion that has distorted your vision, and behold yourself everywhere. Yourself and God are one. Know this and give up all sorrow and fear.

You go to temples and bathe in rivers. You travel for this far and wide. All the while, He whom you seek, the being of bliss and peace, is within you. Your heart is His temple. Your Self, which is God, is dwelling therein. Let the river of your devotion flow. Bathe in such a river and realise Him, within and without. He is yourself.

You live for ever, for you live in all beings and things—in and as every particle and atom. Death is a misnomer. Immortality alone is true. Change does not mean destruction. One is real, all are real. Divinity permeates everything. Divinity is everything.

Search for Him until you are aware that you are He. Let the arrow strike and dissolve in the mark. Let the ray merge in the sun's splendour. Rise above duality. Let your life and God be fused into one!

The Divine Life, p. 55

Ego-Sense Has No Place in Your Life

To realise God is to be God-like; nay, to be God. God is absolute existence, consciousness and bliss. When you know you are immortal, omniscient and everlasting joy, then you have verily realised God. Now your heart is the heart of God, replete with love, forgiveness and compassion.

God being omnipresent, you are now blessed with an equal vision. Your love goes to all alike. Ill will and revenge are not in your nature. You do not seek advantage over others or exploit them. You are aware that you and everyone are one in Spirit; in other words, you behold all beings and creatures as the multiple expressions of your own Self.

You act, as God acts, in a spontaneous manner. Ego-sense has no place in your life. Your vision is single and clear. Your heart is free from all lower passions. You dwell in absolute inner stillness and peace. You are truly an embodiment of the infinite Truth. Your life is a flame, radiating the light of the Eternal. For you there is no high and low, good and bad. In your all-embracing love, none is excluded. You now become a veritable blessing upon this earth.

You have not gained anything new when you have realised God. You were already That. But you have at the moment become conscious of your divine nature which was already yours. The scales have fallen from your eyes. The veil of ignorance is lifted. As the sun shines in all his splendour when he comes out of the clouds, so your life is fully illumined with the glory of God.

Intellectually, you are the light of the world. In feeling, you are omnipresent love. In action, you are the personification of divine energy. In every aspect of your life, you are the expression of the unmanifest, absolute Reality. This is God-vision or Experience.

The Divine Life, pp. 60-61

Evil is Our Own Creation

A Sadhaka should be wide awake, alert and heedful. He should closely watch the movements of his mind to wean it away gradually from the path of ignorance and guide it on the path of knowledge. He should develop a witness-consciousness through meditation and self-surrender. It is a state of awareness of the immortal and radiant Truth within him. In fact, this awareness itself is God-realisation.

All visions of lights and forms have to be transcended before the absolute Reality can be realised. The visions are surely milestones on the spiritual path. But do not cling to them.

Give up doubts and churning of the intellect. Feel you are a simple child of the Lord and thus enter into His being. This is the easy way to reach Him. Do not perplex the mind with questions. Be humble, pure and cheerful, taking refuge in Him. Follow the straight and simple path of devotion. Open the flood-gates of your heart and allow Prem, pure love, that is in you to flow over unimpeded to the holy feet of the Lord seated within. Remember that God's grace is ever with you. Benefit by its redeeming influence, by opening yourself to receive it and becoming aware of the *Amrita Vrishti*—shower of nectar.

Some churning of the mind or intellect may be there. But after some time, this process should stop so that the butter of Divine Bliss may be formed and collected. After the impurities are eliminated, pure and divine emotions rise up. Even this stage is passed when the infinite silence of the inner peace is experienced. Here the rippling and dancing river mingles with the calm waters of the ocean. That is the end of all Sadhana.

You cannot please everybody in the world. When the mind is drawn within and you are absorbed in the Self, you will be unaffected by what people say about you. Be true to the Atman within you.

Cultivate the consciousness that keeps you detached from the mind and its antics. This can be done only be your continued remembrance of the Divine Power that resides in you. Despair and dejection are enemies on the path of spiritual progress. Do not allow the mind to be depressed on any account. Keep yourself cheerful by chanting the Mantra. Your life must flow in a spontaneous and natural way. Your nature should become childlike.

Good and evil are merely conceptual and relative. What is good for you may be bad for another. There are no fixed standards, but only those set by the mind. There is a state beyond the mind in which there is no good and evil. There you see the whole universe filled with the light of the Divine.

What, after all, is right and wrong? That which takes you towards God is right and that which takes you away from God is wrong. There is no question of right and wrong for one who has realised God. He has transcended all duality. His entire life is an offering at the feet of God. His life flows spontaneously for the good of all. For him there is only God, and God is all.

In the eyes of God there is no evil. We suffer because of our ego. The sense of individuality, or separation from others, is responsible for all apparent evils. God is all-benevolent and all-loving. If you think of God constantly you can be happy in all situations. If you can take it that God's will prevails in the world and everything happens by His will you cannot see evil anywhere and there is no suffering for you at any time. This is Ramdas' experience.

Evil is our own creation; it is not God's creation. If we have the vision of God, we cannot see evil anywhere. When love prevails evil disappears. Evil is the offspring of the ignorant mind. If we accept the sovereignty of God by surrendering ourselves to His will, we love all alike and see no evil at all. Just as darkness disappears before light, evil disappears in the light of God.

God never punishes. Punishment is always self-inflicted. We bring suffering on ourselves by our own wrong actions. If we are conscious that God is acting through us, we will never do any wrong. We do wrong only when we forget God.

Everyone has some good points in him. We should see only those good points. If we are to see bad points, let us look for them only in ourselves. If we practise this, the evil in us will disappear. If we see evil in others and good in us, what little of good we have will disappear and the evil in us will grow. By criticizing and thinking ill of others, we only make our minds more and more impure. The way to progress is to see good in everyone and love everyone. To see good in others is to see God in them; for God alone is good. By seeing God in others we can easily realise God in our own heart. So long as we criticise others we can never see God in them.

Adversity is not undesirable. Because, it is only when you are down and out in life that you can realise its true value. Face all the vicissitudes in life by throwing yourselves completely on the mercy of the Almighty Lord. When you are made to go through the fire of suffering, you can come out of it purified and strengthened. Such suffering constitutes real Sadhana for attaining God. The more bitter it is, the more rapid becomes your spiritual progress. God-realisation does not mean living in worldly comfort and opulence. It means living in peace and freedom, whatever the external conditions may be. For such a person misery has no sting. The lives of most of the great saints of the world clearly show that they had the worst of sufferings. When you are disowned by the world you become the acknowledged child of God.

Heroes are they who suffer and sacrifice for the sake of Truth or God. Strange are the ways of the Divine! His most beloved devotees, to whom He reveals Himself in all His glory, are made by Him to pass through great trials and tribulations both before and after they are accepted by Him. Before they realise Him, these sufferings are for their own self-purification and after their realisation, they are for the uplift and redemption of mankind.

Thus Speaks Ramdas, paras 90-103

Faith in God

Faith in God means faith in your own higher Self who is your real being. The main qualities of this faith are absolute fearlessness, and freedom from worry and anxiety of every kind, through a complete surrender in all things to the Almighty will of this supreme Self. To attain to this surrender you have to keep your mind dwelling constantly in God, not permitting it to come down to harassing thoughts about your body and other matters. This highest Truth that resides in you is all compassionate and merciful. What you have to do is to trust this great Truth and give up all cares. Faith can move mountains is a trite saying.

Keep to a life of strict discipline by adjusting your food and rest according to a set system. Above all, maintain strictly a life of Brahmacharya. Merely praying to God without the corresponding effort on your part cannot avail you anything. Life is granted for the achievement of a great ideal which is freedom and cheerfulness in selfless service and sacrifice. The mere dedication of life to this exalted purpose will liberate it from all distempers.

When you have once taken complete refuge in God, you ought to give up all doubts and worries. You have to consider that, whatever way He decides the course of events in your life, it is always for good. Worldly honour and disgrace have no bearing on His decisions. You must freely and unreservedly put yourself in His hands. He can never come to your rescue if you do not cease from worrying and restlessness. Self-surrender means a state of perfect peace and calmness, attained through complete submission to the Divine Will.

Fears and anxieties cannot affect you in all your undertakings, provided you are sure and firm in your faith. God is the great provider and he who trusts Him is never lost. Only you have to tune your will with His will, mingle your consciousness with His divine light and wisdom, merge your life in His eternal existence; then you are perfectly safe in all situations of life.

The divine power manifest and working in great Mahatmas is capable of performing wondrous miracles. By faith alone you could attain high and ambitious ideals. If you are earnestly after spiritual illumination, you must strenuously work for it by concentrating all your thought on the supreme goal of life, the immortal Reality that dwells within you. Merely running after Gurus, without faith and a sincere aspiration for being benefited by their contact, will be of no use.

Glimpses of Divine Vision, pp. 41-44

Faith Works Wonders

As a rudder is an indispensable necessity for the safe-piloting of a boat on the ocean, so faith is to life in the world. Faith can be defined as the unflinching reliance upon an invincible Truth that resides in the heart of a human being. A man without faith is a vacillating creature, vacillating between sorrow and fear, whereas he who possesses faith is the real hero who has conquered weakness and stands firm like a rock in all the storms of life. He not only faces bravely all the shocks that come to him in life but also with an irresistible will triumphs over them. The one predominant quality of faith is fearlessness. The Almighty Power lodged within him is his main refuge. The soul that has this faith is ever sure of his ground, and lives and acts unerringly in agreement with the promptings of the great ideal which he cherishes and adores in his own heart. Such a faith is said to work wonders—wonders, appearing as such, according to the external laws that govern things.

As a certain cause produces an inevitable result, which is true of most things perceptible to the senses, so through faith as the cause certain results are produced, which though seemingly strange, are perfectly natural in the inner workings of nature.

Instead of using the power of faith in trying to mould external affairs, the right use of this power is to effect a transformation of one's entire heart and life.

If there is one being on whom we can put absolute trust, or on whom we can depend at all times and in all conditions, it should be the Supreme Truth. Man's fall from his Divine state is due to his lack of faith in an ultimate Reality. Sterling faith is closely associated with selfless love. The heart is the seat of love, so also the seat of Truth, and Truth and love being one, faith means undoubting confidence in the greatness of Truth.

The Divine Life, p. 110

Gandhi was a Saint or God-Man

Mahatma Gandhi, the outstanding world figure of the day, has departed from our midst. We know that only the physical part of him has perished but that his immortal spirit still abides with us and dwells and will dwell always in the hearts of his admirers and devotees of the present generation and also of the coming generations for ages and ages. Essentially, Mahatma Gandhi was a saint or God-man. He infused in the hearts of his followers, all over the world, faith in God, and led them on the path of divine love, righteousness and truth. His principle of non-violence is nothing but the principle of universal love based on the realisation of the supreme unity of all life on this earth. His deep anxiety for the welfare of humanity, his compassion towards the sufferers, the poor and the downtrodden, his sustained concern in bringing about goodwill, amity and harmony among people who sought to ruthlessly destroy each other's life and property, as displayed in the communal riots, and his untiring effort for the removal of injustice done to the Harijans or the so-called untouchables, mark him out as a benefactor of humanity, unparalleled in the history of the world for many centuries past.

Mahatma Gandhi toiled indefatigably for the good of India in particular and the world at large in general. Everyday it is becoming more and more evident, after the mortal part of him was confined to the flames, that his imperishable spirit is working with a greater intensity, for awakening the world to the consciousness of its inherent unity. While the wave of mourning passes over the world, his ever glowing spirit seems still to inspire and galvanize the hearts of people in different parts of the earth to the awareness of the supreme Truth or God—the one great Master that determines the destinies of the human race. By striving to bring humanity nearer God when walking on the earth, he is yet, after leaving it, subtly working towards the formation of a universal brotherhood. His message of love and truth is producing a greater and more far-reaching effect on the minds of people now than when he was alive in the flesh. He has veritably roused us all to the supreme need of the establishment of peace and goodwill on earth and convinced us that strife, discord and war must disappear from the face of it. Saints of Mahatma Gandhi's spiritual eminence do not die. As a result of the supreme sacrifice which he made, may hatred and ill will be eradicated from the hearts of men all over the world! May mutual love and friendliness prevail so that the entire humanity live together in harmony and peace!

The above tribute to his exalted and illumined soul cannot be complete without making mention of his predominantly devotional nature and unshakeable faith in the name of God. By unbroken communion with the Divine through the practice of Ramnam he became a radiant Vibhuti who dedicated his life for the service of God in humanity. Verily, there is no easier way of linking the soul with God and beholding Him everywhere—in all beings and creatures—than constantly remembering Him by the utterance or singing of His holy and all-powerful Name.

The Divine Life, pp. 191-192

Glorify Him and His Name

Behold! God is within you.

God is infinite Love.
He is the eternal Light and Joy that pervade the whole universe.
Rise above the thought of all mundane things.
Reach the height and glory of God's pure and effulgent presence.
Give up "I" and "mine", and you are face to face with God.

Elevate every thought, and you dwell in a blissful Divine consciousness, i.e. in God.

Aspire to realise God! See Him in the beginning, in the middle, and in the end of all things and happenings.

Be humble, be pure, be simple, be innocent, and God is yours.

God, who is Love, dwells in your heart. Be conscious of this at all times. Then your thoughts are of love, your words are of love, and your acts are of love.

Let the splendour of God ever illumine your heart. Then it is all light for you, inside, outside and everywhere.

Step out of the darkness of ignorance, enter into the light of knowledge, and there stand facing God—the light of all lights.

Let your deeds be the spontaneous works of God within you.

Brush aside pride, and permit God to work in you.

God is the only Reality; God is the only Truth. Know this and live for God alone.

Do not cling to perishable things; make the eternal God your all in all.

If you seek everlasting peace and joy, lay aside your desire for transient things; let no longing but for God fire your bosom.

Don't pursue the shadows; name, fame and glory appear and disappear, ultimately dragging you down to ruin and grief.

Be free from the allurements of lust and gold. These put out the Divine Light within you, and throw you back into darkness and misery.

Bask always in the sunshine of God's splendour and glory.

Do not lose touch of God; be ever in tune with Him.

Be calm and cheerful always.

Let your eyes look with kindliness, your tongue speak with mildness, and your hands touch with softness.

To soothe the aching heart, to infuse courage into the drooping spirit, to bring a smile upon the face pale with woe, to assuage sorrow by loving words, are the works of a God-lover.

Offer your all to God, and then be His true servant.

Beware of conceit and self-praise.

Remember, He within you is doing all.

Glorify Him and His Name.

Distinctions of caste, creed, colour and race are false. All are one in God.

Behold God in all; love Him in all, serve Him in all, be one with all.

The God in your heart is the God that dwells in all. Your union with Him means your union with all.

Realise that God is the doer.

Surrender your ego to Him.

Give up your individual will; make God's will your will.

Surrender gives you love, peace and joy—manifests God within you.

Resist not evil. Return good for evil. Forgive, forgive,

forgive—be this the motto of your life.

God's love is forgiveness and compassion itself.

Purify your heart so that God may take His seat in you.

There is no greater virtue than humility, no vice greater than pride.

Give up show and hypocrisy.

The flower of God blossoms in you—only in the atmosphere of innocence and sincerity.

Leave the world alone; yours is to find Him and Him alone.

Be absorbed in the thought of God. Be ever immersed in God-consciousness, in a state of transcendent bliss and peace.

Be ever watchful; make God your helper, friend and mother.

Don't despair in failure and fall. God's grace is upon you.

Seek His aid. He is Almighty. Complete surrender He demands of you; then only will He make you His own.

Permit God to change you, mould you as He wills. He enlightens and makes you conscious of your identity with Him.

You are at once one with God and different from Him.

In Spirit all are one; in bodies there is diversity. All bodies and forms are the Spirit's manifestation. This is the Divine Unity in variety and multiplicity.

Remember God always, if you would surrender to Him.

Make the mansion of God's holiness your permanent abode.

Be like the flower: give out always the perfume of love and joy.

Pray that always you may be in Him and He in you, i.e. to grant you this awareness.

He is always in you and you are in Him, whether you know it or not.

Nothing is yours; everything is God's; do not forget this!

You have come from God, and you are on your way to Him.

Walk the path of saints and sages. Know that the path is the goal.

Even when you are walking the path, you have reached the destination.

Realise that you are the immortal Spirit.

Cast away fear, doubt and anxiety.

Give up all plans, schemes and expectations of the future.

Every minute is pregnant with joy in communion with God.

Knowledge dawns; and you see God's presence in you and with you.

As the chickens feel secure beneath the wings of the mother-hen, so be at peace under the protecting influence of God who is your Divine Mother.

The Divine Life, pp. 144-146

God-Experience is the Highest Acquisition

God-perception or God-experience is the highest acquisition of human life. God is in our very breath. Our eyes behold God everywhere. Our nose smells Him. Our tongue tastes Him. Our ears hear Him and hands touch Him. He lives in our thoughts and feelings and acts. So, every moment we dwell in His all-pervading presence, nay, each one of us is a veritable embodiment of Divinity. There is nothing but He. Without Him, nothing can exist, as with Him everything does.

As the Cosmic Force, it is He who controls everything. It is by His light the sun, the moon and all luminous bodies shine. The worlds and the universes are His self-revelations. When this supreme vision is attained, what words can describe the beauty, power and glory of God?

The chief condition to achieve Him, to realise our perfect identity with Him, and to enjoy eternal bliss and freedom, is to dissolve the individual sense that bars us from attaining this beatific state.

It is the sense of separation from Him that has built the wall between man and Him. This is the veil of Maya or nescience. This separation has to be pulled down. Then the aspirant and God become one. The drop mingling in the ocean becomes ocean itself. The individual realises that He is the Cosmic Truth and Being.

This sublime consummation can be brought about by the easy method of self-surrender. Self-surrender is effected by tuning the mind, which is the cause of producing the illusion of separateness, to the one single thought of God. The heart involved in the attraction and attachment for the objects of the moment should offer all its love and adoration to Him. Life in all its channels should flow for His sake. It should be in all respects permeated, enveloped and inspired through and through by the one consciousness of God.

Again it must be definitely said that this is the *summum bonum* of human life. This is the goal.

The Divine Life, pp. 40-41

God Has Revealed Himself in Me

Renunciation is expansion. The love that I once gave to a few I now give to all. Thus have I attained a freedom by which I know I am immortal.

My love is strangely based upon my identity with all beings and things. There is no separation. Diversity is appearance. It is but unity manifest as the many. When I love one, I love all. One and all mean the same.

God has revealed Himself in me. His effulgence fills me through and through. My life is an overflowing stream of ecstasy.

I bask in the light of my Being. I see myself everywhere. I am stillness, infinite, yet in me there is a motion—vibrant and harmonious. God only is. I am He—all are He!

I rest in God. Who am I? In what language can I speak of Him who is my own Self? I am His eternal companion. How can I express the joy I get in communion with Him?

When the day dawns and the tiny birds, flitting from one branch to another of the mango-grove, are singing sweetly, I sit entranced, conscious of my oneness with the dawn, birds, trees and all nature.

I live on the plane of non-duality. Truly there is only one plane, if it can be called a plane at all. There are no planes, no states and no stages. It is all one whole, one perfection, one indivisible Truth. I am lost in ecstasy transcending all diversity.

What is Self-realisation? It is giving up the pretension that you are not the Self, that you are a mere body. People say to me, "You are God Himself." I reply, "You are also He." "We are not He"—they rejoin. What else is this, but that they simulate and, for some Lila of their own, hide behind a mask their real and divine nature?

Great teachers and saints tell us God is in our own heart and we are His temple. They also say the temple is Himself. So we are all He in totality, in all aspects of life, a perfect image of His. This is the Truth.

The Divine Life, pp. 59-60

God is a Living Reality

God is a living reality. He is more real than the ephemeral interests and things in which man is usually involved. Man's craving for the earthly achievements shuts him out from the recognition of the immortal truth of his existence. He is so deeply caught in the pleasures which are gained through mere sense perception and touch that he becomes blind to the exalted experience of eternal bliss and peace.

Divine nectar he rejects and seeks for satisfaction in transient delights which are ever accompanied with the reaction of acute pain and sorrow.

The question that troubles everyone who has turned his back to the light of God is, "Which is the way out?" When asked to turn his face to the supreme Light, he replies, "None of your devotion, God and immortality to me. Give me something which will yield pleasure to my senses and intellect. Change your strain to suit my fancy. At any rate do not talk too much of Bhakti. I find no relish for it."

So God who is the very abode of absolute peace and happiness is not wanted. The loving God of his heart speaks aloud and says "O, My child, you can have no peace and freedom until you find them in Me. By taking refuge in Me alone can you achieve the fulfilment of your burning quest of life. Your struggling river of life should mingle with the ocean of My eternal life." The message from the Divinity within is unheard and unrealised. And man thus moves ceaselessly in a whirl of cares, anxieties, fears and doubts.

So, O beloved soul, unless you link your life with the Divine author of your being, your life is in vain. The earth gave you birth as human being so that you might attain to the knowledge of your Divine existence. Shun the lower planes and soar up to the height of immortality. By complete self-surrender permit the supreme Lord seated in your heart to reveal Himself in all His glory.

The Divine Life, p. 12

God is Absolute Joy

Joy is the aim of all beings and creatures on this earth. Of these a human being alone can know the secret source from which joy of all kinds emanate. In fact even the delight experienced through the senses has its root in this hidden source which we call God, who dwells within us. God is absolute joy, and from Him have projected all the principles of manifestation. Just as to know the seed is to know the tree, so also to know the root cause of the world-manifestation which is God, is to know the nature of the manifestation. We can therefore infer that the universe, being the expression of God, is made up of waves of joy.

In a human being, every part of him, subtle or gross, is a concrete expression of eternal joy—even the momentary pleasures and pains are ripples on the ocean of infinite joy. So, everywhere there is nothing but the forms of joy, because everything is God who is joy.

When the devotee has realised the full splendour of God and is surcharged with ecstasy, and has merged in Him, he cannot contain himself. He dances, being seized with a rare rapture, his entire body thrilling with bliss. The very name and thought of God sets him ablaze, as it were, with this exalted experience. In this state the line of demarcation that divides the devotee and his God disappears and God reveals Himself as the devotee.

Where this supreme joy is at play, there, love rises in floods. Here all diversity and distinctions dissolve into the supreme

Spirit, who is the sole Truth and than whom there is none other.

The experience of the devotee in this attainment does not admit of description, as language is utterly incapable of doing so. He who enjoys it alone knows what it is.

India has presented to the world a galaxy of saints who have reached the heights of such Divine ecstasy mentioned above. All of them are the veritable embodiments of devotion of the highest type. They have poured out the joy of their souls in their songs and teachings. Love is their theme and joy their strain. He who has drunk the nectar, which they yield, has sweetened his life for ever and ever.

The Divine Life, pp. 19-20

God is Behind Everything

The only way to be always happy is to submit to God's will, and leaving everything to Him, to be contented in the condition in which He places us. Surrender means inner contentment and peace. It means giving up of the ego-sense. Until the ego-sense is completely eliminated, we cannot realise God.

Self-surrender means that we throw the whole burden of life, our anxieties and sorrows on the Supreme Lord who is the Master of all and keep our mind filled with calmness and peace that comes from His constant remembrance.

Cling to the Lord in all situations. Do not worry about anything. Have complete trust in God. Give up all superstitious notions. Do not mind the opinions of the world about you. Court the society of pure and noble souls. Whenever changes come in your life, take them that they come by God's will alone. Take to the changes naturally and cheerfully.

We are ever under God's care and protection. We are never forsaken. God is all love. We have doubts about this because we are not conscious of His love. Let us know once and for all that He is our sole refuge. We are ever watched over, guided and lovingly taken care of by Him. So let us surrender ourselves to Him, keeping up His remembrance always.

Surrender to God as you are. It is not that we must purify ourselves first and then go to Him. He must purify us. We must go to Him as a child to its mother. If the child goes to her in a dirty condition, the mother does not turn it away nor ask it to come clean. She herself takes the child and bathes it clean. God is more loving than the earthly mother.

When we surrender to God and allow ourselves to be guided by Him, all 'obstacles' that come on the way are found to be helpful and beneficial to our progress. Life is a battle for all. There is joy in winning as well as losing in this battle. Let your heart be ever in tune with God. Then winning and losing are seen as the play of the Divine.

Some persons say that surrender is a sign of weakness. Ramdas says it is the path of the strong. Surrender is not so easy as people seem to think. It is very hard to eradicate the ego-sense. Surrender is the only way to root out the ego. It is the straight path that leads to God.

Really, man has no will of his own. There is only one Divine will at work everywhere and in all. It is a mistake to think that we, as individuals, have got any power to do anything. God is behind everything. His power does all things. If we know that His power is alone active in us and submit to Him, we shall be free from the ego-sense and realise that we are the infinite, universal Spirit.

Know once and for all that, as an individual actor, you do not exist. It is the one Divine Shakti or Power that controls and guides all movements and changes in the world. You are the instrument actuated by God's power; you are the very expression of God—nay, you are God Himself!

Thus Speaks Ramdas, paras 43-51

God is the Friend of the Helpless

No human being in this world can say that he has not the moments of acute depression, harrowing sense of loss, blankness of despair and pangs of agony, suspense and utter grief. In these crucial moments he has sought a way to escape from the painful condition to which he is subjected. He looks for some hand strong enough to lift him out of his slough of despondency. His aching heart cries for help but he receives no response from anywhere. His crest-fallen spirit sinks lower still. His so-called friends, relations and fellow-men in the world fail him. Who could then save him and grant him peace? Where is hope for him? Then like a flash the words of saints and devotees of God rush into his mind. Yes, there is one great hope, there is one great refuge, there is one great saviour—and He is God.

God is the friend of the helpless and the shelter of the weak and the suffering. He is the protector and nourisher of the world. He is the most loving parent of all beings and creatures. You do not appeal to Him in vain. The instant you turn your face to Him and long to be folded in His loving embrace, that instant He pours on you the soothing light of His infinite grace. Your heavy-laden heart is at once unloaded of its sorrow. Your mind is bathed in the nectar of peace. Your soul, like a bird set free, now sings the song of freedom and joy. You feel intuitively that you have now come under the protection of an all-powerful being. You become conscious that He is ever with you, in you, about you, watching, guiding and guarding you with the most loving vigilance and care.

Such is the experience of many a saint and devotee of the past and the present. Such is the experience of Ramdas who writes these lines. Really, there is no safer and surer refuge for a creature than the supreme Lord of the universe. Remember this Lord and feel always humble and childlike before Him. Offer yourself entirely to Him and enjoy for ever and ever the blessings of true peace and freedom. Love Him beyond all the things and objects. Hold Him as your all in all. He is in your heart.

Those who turn to God with perfect trust and confidence are always filled with peace and joy. They are free from all sorts of cares and worries.

The Divine Life, pp. 12-13

God Wants a Heart Longing for Him Alone

Religion is not a subject for discussion, much less for speculation. Religion means re-union of the soul with the Lord. It signifies the intimate relationship between the two. This relationship develops into an uninterrupted communion with Him. Such communion and the resultant purity and peace can be had by anybody and at any place.

God wants us to be pure in heart. It is only then we can see Him and realise Him. He does not mind whether we go to this church or that, this temple or that, whether we belong to any particular creed, society or organisation. What He wants is a heart longing for Him alone. So it is an individual concern. God is open to all. He is like the free air which all can breathe. His presence can be felt everywhere, whether it be in the church, temple, market place, office, caves or jungles.

God is the Beloved of our heart. The condition to be fulfilled before we can have Him is the attainment of a guileless, pure and innocent nature. Only when His grace flows into our life, we are transfigured. He should accept us and we are saved. This is the simple way to have Him. Theology and philosophy are big things for those who are wise and learned.

The Divine Life, p. 370

Grace is Ever Pouring on Us from God

God has made the law of Karma, but He can also set it aside. If He cannot brush aside His law, the law will be greater than He. This cannot be. For, He is the infinite, omnipotent Lord. So He must have the power to suspend any law. Generally God does not interfere. He allows the Karma to be worked out. But He may, in special cases, go beyond His law and by His grace free the soul from the bondage of Karma.

Our mind turns towards God only by His grace. It is His grace that makes us yearn for Him. Grace is self-revealing. When Grace comes to us, our heart becomes perfectly pure and we overflow with love for all beings. We shall have no ill-feeling towards anybody. We shall experience a rare joy which we never had before.

Does faith come first or Grace first? It has been conclusively proved by saints who have had the highest spiritual experience that Grace comes first. Without Grace we cannot have faith in God. The true devotee says: "Oh God I remember You because You remembered me first."

Our ego-sense makes us think we can attain Him by our Sadhana or struggle. But we soon realise our helplessness and know that our efforts are by themselves of no avail. Then we surrender to Him and depend on His mercy. Thus we need His grace at the beginning, in the middle and at the end. Grace is all in all.

We cannot get Grace by virtue of our so-called merit. The worst sinners have received Grace and become pure and glorious. Purity is not a condition precedent for Grace. It is the flow of Grace that makes the heart pure. When Grace comes, it comes, not because we deserve it, nor as a reward for our Sadhana, but only out of God's boundless mercy and love.

One who gets Grace never feels he is worthy of it.

The way of Grace is mysterious. You struggle for it and you do not get it. Sometimes, without any struggle, you get it. Its working is governed by something beyond all laws. It is not bound by any rules, regulations or conditions. You are wonderstruck when Grace comes to apparently undeserving persons, while the so-called deserving ones are still waiting for it.

Looked at from another angle, it must be said Grace is pouring on all alike. Some receive it and some do not. Some people open the windows of their hearts to receive Grace and benefit by it while others keep them closed and so they do not get it. But even to keep the windows of the heart open, we require inner aspiration and longing which can come to us only through His grace.

Grace is ever pouring on us from God, as the sun is ever shedding light on all objects—opaque, translucent and transparent. But opaque objects do not reflect the light, translucent things reflect it but partially, while transparent things reflect it fully. The difference is not due to the absence or failure of sunlight, but due to the difference in the reflecting capacity of the objects. Similarly, we imbibe Grace and benefit by it according to our capacity to receive, according to our preparedness and purity.

If Grace is all in all, and comes of its own accord, governed by no laws and conditions, what is the place of Sadhana in spiritual life? Why should we perform Sadhana at all? The secret is that Sadhana is done to make us realise that by Sadhana alone we cannot attain Him. So long as our ego-sense persists we cannot see God. When we know we are utterly helpless in spite of all our efforts to attain Him, our ego-sense is crushed and we throw ourselves at His feet.

It is difficult to know why God reveals Himself to some and plays the game of hide-and-seek with others. It is His Lila. He cannot be accused of favouring some and forsaking others. Let us always remember that He ever dwells in us and that we ever dwell in Him. He who reveals Himself to us is He. He who plays hide-and-seek with us is also He. Everything is He. Guru is He, Sishya is He, Player is He, Witness is He. There is none but He. Realise this great truth and rest happy.

Thus Speaks Ramdas, paras 60-69

Grace is Sure to Descend

The way of elevating human life is from its lower plane to the higher, from a state of ignorance to one of knowledge, from the consciousness of the individual to the consciousness of the universal, in short, from the conditioned and limited to the unconditioned and infinite, is at once most easy and most difficult. It is not merely our earnest endeavour for the realisation of the supreme Reality of our nature that is sufficient, but the power of the Divine grace should pour on us spontaneously in order to produce the needed Divine transformation.

The secret of the great change by which the entrapped soul of man is liberated into the all-blissful realisation of immortality—the conditions necessary for the consummation of this task—is a supreme mystery. After deeply considering this question from every possible avenue, it has been decisively arrived at that the power of will that could effect a momentous transfiguration of life into its Divine essence lies entirely with the Almighty Controller of all worlds and beings and creatures and things in them. This great original Spirit with a silent and irresistible force from within the human soul, unravels its own magnificent glory, unfailing bliss and all-embracing love.

If we could, by the help of our reasoning faculties, try to build a system of thought to understand the meaning and conditions governing it, we can say, for realising the absolute unity of the individual soul with the infinite cosmic Spirit, it is incumbent upon the soul who aspires to be blessed with this beatific state that he ought to, on his part, possess himself with a burning aspiration for the realisation of his real spiritual eminence. Given this condition, it is contended that Divine grace is sure to descend on him changing him into a being of eternal splendour and joy. The above condition is held to be a necessary criterion for the attainment of the eternal Divine life, but still instances can be quoted wherein Divine grace worked miraculously on the least prepared souls, granting them the knowledge and joy of the Divine. Individual effort and initiative, so far as spiritual evolution is concerned, appears to be futile in the absence of the Divine grace which alone should work in the heart of man and automatically drive him on the path of spirituality. And then rising from stage to stage, he should ultimately reach the all-transcendent and supreme Reality. The devotee rightly says: "O God, I should not have remembered Thee if Thou hadst not first remembered me." So, God in His infinite mercy selects souls in the world irrespective of their fitness or otherwise for converting them into channels for the manifestation of His infinite power, light and glory granting them the knowledge of His cosmic existence. So the soul that sincerely wishes to dwell in the Divine and become one with Him should wait patiently like the proverbial bird, which longs to drink the cool brilliance of the full moon, for that psychological moment to arrive. This period of waiting can be best utilised by being in the presence of those great souls whom the grace of the Lord has converted into His very images. Here his hunger finds the food to appease it to a considerable extent, because the society of Mahatmas reveals to the soul the great purpose of his birth and existence, and raises him to the consciousness of his immortality.

The Divine Life, pp. 131-132

Grace of a Saint

It is essential for a devotee, who is keen upon realising the infinite love of God, to receive the touch and grace of a saint. It is through the transmitting power of an illuminated soul that the aspirant is awakened to the reality of his true and higher life which is union and oneness with God. It is only by such contact that the devotee is able to maintain a continual stream of God-remembrance in his mind.

A saint is he who is an embodiment of divine love, wisdom and power. He is God Himself manifest in flesh and blood. He is at once Guru and God. To adore him is to worship the highest Reality dwelling in our hearts. He is the great redeemer and saviour of all fallen souls. The grace of a saint converts an erring and ignorant mortal into a being full of wisdom, love and joy.

We become that which we constantly contemplate. If we keep a great personal ideal of a saint before us and through faith and reverence tune our life and spirit with his life and spirit, we are gradually moulded into the likeness of the great soul. It must be understood that we should not merely cling to the external form of our accepted spiritual ideal, but we should realise within ourselves the immortal Spirit which is revealed in the Guru.

In order to receive a saint's grace that transmutes us into the Divine, we should fully open ourselves to his regenerating influence. Before the saint, we must be as humble as a blade of grass and as simple and innocent as a child. Our trust and refuge in him must be entire and complete. Given this condition, the saint's grace is sure to pierce through us, destroying the darkness of ignorance, and enlighten our hearts with the glory and sublimity of divine love and peace. It is then that the thought of God will permeate our mind so much so that it will send a current of ecstasy coursing through every atom of our physical and psychical being. Love, light and joy will now radiate through us. We shall realise the presence of God everywhere. We will lose ourselves in the ineffable bliss born of our dwelling totally in the Lord and ultimately merge our individuality in the cosmic light of our beloved Master, Mother and Lord—the supreme Love who is God.

This is the summit of divine attainment to which a saint's grace leads the struggling soul. Therefore, let all who aspire for eternal love, bliss, power and wisdom seek first the society of saints and by their contact be reborn into a new life surcharged with an infinite vision.

The Divine Life, pp. 154-155

Gurus Awaken the Dormant Spirit

On the question of the necessity of a Guru there is amongst many people a good deal of speculation. Some of them assert with vehemence that a Guru is not at all necessary for the spiritual progress of an aspirant, and that his own personal effort is sufficient; others, with equal emphasis declare, that no spiritual progress in an individual, however hard he may strive for himself, can be possible except through the grace and guidance of a Guru. Before we discuss this important subject, it is essential in the first place to understand the true significance of the term "Guru".

Guru is understood to be the awakener of the dormant spirit of the aspirant to the consciousness of the immortal Self or God. Guru is the guide and the leader. Guru is the Truth personified. Guru imparts the knowledge of the highest Truth, leading the thought of the aspirant to the comprehension of the deathless life. Guru is he whose life has mingled with God's life, who is intoxicated with the bliss of the eternal and whose heart is overflowing with compassion and love for all creatures and beings in the world. The touch, society or even a sight of such a great and illumined personality would at once bring a sense of indescribable relief to the struggling soul, and set him on the path of immortality, peace and bliss. What does the Guru say to the soul in tribulation? He exhorts: "Go within yourself and behold therein the splendour and glory of the eternal Truth. Therein resides your ultimate home of perfect release, happiness and peace. Therein find the life that never fades, that never changes but ever blesses and sanctifies. Be in tune with that

Reality, if you sincerely crave for the highest consummation of life." It is thus the Guru awakens you, and thereafter you are always awake. This is the real conception of a Guru.

It is admitted on all hands that development on the physical and mental planes requires the aid of a proficient guide or master. This is the law of nature holding true in all cases of mental and physical revival and progress of mankind. To flout or deny this universal law only in matters spiritual is to deliberately ignore the lessons which his or her own experiences have held out. From the time the child is born until it departs this life, having passed through its various stages of growth to old age, it does inevitably become both the teacher and the taught. He who argues against the need of a teacher invariably assumes the role of a teacher himself. This is a paradox which he alone would be able to explain if he could.

It is an incontestable fact that a great mother, a great professor or expert or a great saint is responsible for the enlightenment of the heart, head and soul of a human being. If we, with a clear vision, study the lives of all the great men and women of the world, past or present, we cannot fail to observe that a dominant power for good at the back of them had influenced and moulded their career. Sometimes, this power may have acted in such a subtle and mysterious manner that the recipients of it could hardly have recognised it. These cases of non-recognition are happily very few. It is these that contend that a Guru or a spiritual teacher is a superfluity. Based on this averment, many ignorant people, who have neither the initiative nor the humility for the spiritual adventure, parrot-like repeat the words of the above masters. They forget that by so doing they are also blindly and unconsciously accepting these great ones as their teachers. But those who are distinctly alive to the transforming influence of a great Soul on them, which brought about a permanent change in their angle of vision from the ephemeral to the eternal values of life, boldly declare that without the healing and elevating touch of a spiritual teacher there is no hope for the deluded soul.

The Divine Life, pp. 115-117

The Heart is Really a Temple of God

When the heart becomes pure and is awakened to the consciousness of the Divine, the entire human vehicle reflects His light in all its constituents. The body, mind and senses then are permeated with this light. The person so blessed becomes truly a luminous expression of God. The spiritual radiance that goes out from him or her is cool like the rays of the moon and it elevates and heals the mentally diseased souls who come in contact with it. God reveals Himself in all His splendour in the heart of such a great one.

How does a person attain to this transcendent light and joy? The one and the only way is self-surrender, born of complete absence of egoism. By this alone the divine power and glory are made manifest in a human being. The heart is really a temple of God when one recognises this and is aware of it. A person reveals his or her inner power and glory when the intellect is illumined with the light of God, the heart responds to the eternal symphony of love and the physical body pours out, spontaneously, energy, translating itself into divine action. The person is now no longer egoistic in his or her outlook and activity, but is a vibrant instrument of the Divine, living and moving for the uplift and welfare of the world. The influence such a person casts over humanity and all creation is wonderful.

God is light and joy. God is love and wisdom. God is the supreme power that controls all the world. Such a God dwells in the hearts of us all. To realise Him is the supreme purpose and the goal of life. All else is of no importance or avail.

God is a reality. He is our intimate friend. It is by constant association with Him that we experience our oneness with Him. We start to reach Him as separate from Him, but ultimately the fusion between us and Him becomes so complete that duality disappears and we stand revealed as He Himself. Confusing diversity then gives place to absolute unity.

So long as we feel apart from Him, our life is beset with many an obstruction and we are subject to all kinds of cramping and unhappy vicissitudes. But when life is released from the bondage of its own making, manifesting its inherent spiritual power, light and grace, then it comes to its own and enjoys everlasting peace and bliss. The life becomes a light to itself and to all others. It is self-revealed and the magnificence of it is past thought and expression. May such a light spread all over the world and may humanity be blessed with the vision of it, and love and harmony prevail on the earth!

The Divine Life, pp. 42-43

Hinduism is a Universal Religion

Religion means to bind back. We have separated ourselves from God and we have to bind ourselves back to Him. This is what is meant by religion. Let us therefore unite ourselves in the name of God, serve one another and live in harmony and peace.

In a house, when there is unity among all members, there is happiness. When they are divided and quarrelling, there is misery. God is the unifying force. Let us seek and find Him.

Man depends upon wealth and glory—the so-called good things—for his joy. These are illusive. The joy you derive from them is like a flicker. Next second, the light is gone and you are enveloped by darkness. But the Divine joy is pure and holy—not a tinge of grief in it—for it is dependent on itself. When you depend upon something else for your joy, and that something disappears, your joy also disappears. If you depend upon the Eternal for joy, it will be for ever. God exists by Himself. He is His own source. If you commune with Him you will have immortal joy.

It is not external circumstances that make us happy or unhappy but it is our internal state and our outward attitude to circumstances. In the *Bhagavad Gita* there is a Sloka which says:

> "Alike in pleasure and pain, who dwells in the self, to whom a clod of earth, stone and gold are alike, to whom the dear and the undear are alike, who is firm,

> the same in censure and praise—(he is said to have crossed beyond the Gunas.)"

This is the state which is held out as the highest in the *Bhagavad Gita*. You have to transcend the pairs of opposites. Otherwise you are like a scared animal at the sacrificial altar. You are afraid at every moment that something bad is in store for you. But you are in a state of equipoise, if you are one with God. Do not strive to get things from outside. Then you will be satisfied with what God gives you. Contentment is a perpetual feast. It can come to you only when you have got the self-existent bliss. It is there already in your heart. You have to be conscious of it. This happens only by His grace. God's radiance, beauty, manifests in you by your chanting His name. By constant remembrance of Him you can purify yourselves and be fit for His vision.

The Hindu religion is a universal religion. It accepts all the great Teachers and spiritual Masters of the world as equally great, because they are all representations or manifestations of the Divine. The Hindus offer equal reverence to Jesus, Mohammed, Zoroaster, Buddha, Krishna or Rama. These are the great Teachers of the world. Hinduism is not an exclusive religion as many other religions are, which claim that people can attain salvation only if they follow their particular Master. But this is not the claim of Hinduism. It says: "All religions are true. You may follow any religion you like but be sincere and look upon the Master, the supreme personality of your religion, as the very expression of Divinity, even as the Masters of other religions are. By having complete faith in your Master you will be saved, whether it be Buddha, Krishna, Jesus or Mohammed." This is the thing you find peculiar in Hinduism

The ideal of Universal Love and Service means that, although we belong to different nationalities and countries, we are essentially one in Spirit. East, west, south and north have no significance in the realm of the Spirit.

The Divine Life, pp. 146-148

Humility Leads to Self-Surrender

Humility is a virtue which forms the basis for a life filled with supreme peace and usefulness. The humility spoken of here is not an outcome of weakness and ignorance, but is born of strength and wisdom. The mighty power of God selects only such instruments for its great works as are gifted with meekness and simplicity.

Truth humility does, indeed, wield a marvellous power for good. If we even cursorily glance through the history of the world, we find that pure and humble souls have been the greatest benefactors of mankind. A humble and unassuming life yields peace and freedom to him who espouses it, whereas a life founded upon pride and self-adulation is a home of misery and bondage. Whilst the one ennobles and elevates human existence, the other vitiates and degrades it.

Joyful service, beneficial to all, is born from this great quality of the human heart—humility. True service is possible only when the self-conscious individual loses his egoistic sense of "actorship" by merging his self-interest in the common weal and welfare of the world. Now his life-interest is identical with the interest of all. This exalted humility can be achieved by realising the eternal fact that an omnipotent power, which is inherent in all creatures and beings, is actuating the individual life and all its actions.

Humility leads to self-surrender, i.e. an attitude of submission to the will and purpose of God, who is the source of infinite power that controls all the movements in the universe. Thus humility lifts the soul from its narrow view and field of life into its real, vast and illumined sphere of existence. Life now flows out in blissful service with all the spontaneity of a water-spring from the side of a mountain.

To attain this felicitous humility, you have to be ever conscious of the Divine will and plan in all matters and events. The life thus liberated is blessed with ineffable delight and ecstasy. Verily, the soul that is humble has alone entrance into the kingdom of immortality.

The Divine Life, pp. 104-105

I am That

There is a charm, a magic power, in Thy name. It catches hold of people and turns them into Gods.

Thy name roots out all desires and bestows immortal peace and joy. The darkness of the soul is dispelled by Thy name flooding it with divine illumination.

What is it that Thy name cannot do? All good things flow from it. When Thy name enters the heart of the miser, he becomes a benefactor of the world. It transforms the cruel man into an image of compassion. Thy name removes hate from the heart, infusing love. It awakens the soul and drives off torpor and ignorance. Where there is narrowness of outlook, Thy name grants universal vision.

When Thy name, sung by Thy devotees, rings in my ears, I am not only thrilled, but my entire being is filled with ecstasy. Oh! What power is in Thy name! Saints sing its glory tirelessly. And I, thy child, attune my tiny voice with theirs in extolling Thy name. Thy name is the sole sustainer of my life. It nourishes my heart and mind. It sends thrills through every vein and tissue of my physical being.

What more can I say? It has moulded me into Thy likeness, into Thy form and spirit. All victory and glory be to Thy name!

Thy name destroys misery and yields unending joy. I became the votary of Thy name and was blessed beyond measure.

Thy name is Thyself, Thy very form, life and being. I am saturated with Thy name and have become Thyself—the resplendent Truth—the goal of seekers. I am That!

The Divine Life, p. 52

I am the Still All-Pervading Spirit

The life that thrills in me vibrates all through the universe. I am the still, all-pervading Spirit. Yet, I move in waves of delight and ride on their crest at the same time.

God is a cosmic presence and that is myself. I am conscious that I am everything. Still, strangely, I am a calm detached witness, unaffected, the ever-glowing Truth.

As God is all in all, He is Love. Love is the light of the oneness of all life. I try to know what is Love and I am lost and become that Love itself. I cannot speak about anything or anybody without feeling I am all that.

I am seized with an intoxication in which there is no duality or diversity. Under this influence, my pen traces on paper these effusions. My cosmic power causes it to move, pouring out my entire being in words of mystic splendour.

Rain falls and I am in its every drop. I am permeating the cool breeze. Oh, what and where am I not?

I and you are false. There is only one truth and that is God. I am bewitched by seeing my beauty everywhere. My 'I' is He, the one God. When I write, it is He who writes.

There is no end to my ecstasies. I am ecstasy. O words, how you delude me! Words are He. Delusion is He.

My power dwells in the luminous heights of space, in the vastness of mid-air and in the blooming earth. Are they all different from me? No. Yet, I write seemingly to puzzle myself.

Verily, I am the greatest puzzle. One thing I can definitely say of myself. I am all love, compassion and smiles.

When I see myself, I see the cosmos. I am the cosmos. When you see yourself, you see the cosmos. You are the cosmos. So, I and you are one. Oh joy! Oh blessedness!

The Divine Life, pp. 208-209

I am Thyself

My Beloved's kindness came to me like the cool rays of the moon. It released me from bondage and healed my sorrows. What a magic touch! What miraculous change!

Now life flows in a blissful stream, glistening with the light of the Beloved. What a vision! The worlds are the forms of my Beloved. He is at once visible and invisible—the Supreme Being and non-being.

I wished Him to stand before my inner sight as an image of unsurpassed beauty—with smile on the face, compassion in the eyes, and love pouring out of Him. Lo! He is there before me, the enchanting Love of my heart.

When the thought of Thee, like a star, sparkles in the sky of my mind, I am lost in Thee, O Lord! The rapture I feel then is beyond compare. This rapture turns me finally into Thyself—raising me beyond all duality.

Thy glory, my Beloved, is seen everywhere. All objects and beings sing paeans to Thy greatness. I go near a tree and its green leaves chant of Thee. I look up to the sky, Oh! it opens out the blue veil and reveals Thy fascination.

A child comes to me—the little living figure of Thy love—and I am charmed. I clasp it in my arms. I lean my head touching its head. Thrills and thrills! It talks, dropping sweetness at every word. Honey is insipid in comparison. O God of love, all hail to Thee!

The enthralling strains of music that fall into my eager ears are surcharged with celestial symphony, the essence of Thyself—my life and soul Thy feet, O my Beloved, be ever on my head and I melt away in Thee!

I tell the scented flower that nods its head in the mild breeze—"Blessed art thou, little beauty, for thou revealest the face of my Beloved." It looks up and seems to smile.

Holiness and sanctity permeate all. My Beloved is everywhere. The entire nature is He. No God for me apart from nature. He covers all and is above all. I sought Him and became one with Him. I loved Him and became love itself. He shines in my eyes. My breath is fragrant with His breath. I move, because He moves. He is wonderful.

I prayed to be mad of Thee. The prayer granted, I have become so. Thou hast totally possessed me. Now I have none but Thee. My entire being is vibrant with Thy love, light and bliss. Truly, I am no longer myself. I am Thyself! One alone exists—either Thyself or myself.

The Divine Life, pp. 53-54

I Live in Ecstasy Always

I am the life of all lives, I am the power of all powers. I am greater than the greatest, smaller than the smallest—I am simply wonderful. To wonder at myself with all the highest power of my imagination is to merge into the wonderful Being and become a wonder myself.

I live in ecstasy always, I live in ecstasy always. I try to find out who is this 'I'—who is this 'I'. "Who am I?" Answer is what? Silence is the answer by which I come to know what the 'I' signifies. In the silence it is—there is no such thing as 'I' or 'you'—in silence it is.

Joy thrills and thrills every fibre of my being, every atom of my frame is dancing with joy, from every pore of my being I am oozing out nothing but pure and unalloyed joy. To die in this state in not death. It is something beyond death and life. It is the state of perennial ecstasy, everlasting bliss, eternal bliss—changeless, ever remaining the same and same. There is one song—one strain that is sung—that is heard—and that is the symphony of joy—the music of true delight.

In the abundance of overflowing joy, I speak. My words are varied expressions of joy. All that I talk begins in joy, moves in joy and ends in joy. In the stillness of my body, in the activity of all its members, in the cessation and movement of my mind and intellect there is—there is all joy—joy. My objectless laughter is the best definition of that joy. I am at all times intoxicated with a joy which I cannot describe—which I cannot describe.

The Divine Life, pp. 68-69

Immortality is the Birth-Right of Mankind

Religion is the bed-rock on which a true regeneration of mankind can be brought about. But this should bear all the characteristics of a universal religion based on the teachings of the great Masters from whose lips flowed the same wisdom and truth. Narrow dogmatism, blind superstitions and outworn traditions, which have blurred the pristine light of spiritual culture through the years, must be shed.

Real happiness depends on a well-ordered society based on moral and spiritual values. True religion should unite man and man through the realisation of the same indwelling Spirit in all. God has no caste. Castes and creeds are of our making. All differences and distinctions which, through the eye of ignorance, one beholds in this variegated world-show, disappear in the exalted, universal vision of the Divine.

The world is at present passing through a crisis. The old civilisation is crumbling to pieces. There is going on a reshuffling of the values of life. The lesson that the present situation holds for mankind is that unbridled lust for power and possession leads to strife and war, that selfishness, greed and pride, whether among individuals or nations, cause widespread suffering and misery. Out of the travails through which the world is passing, a new order is bound to emerge based on a knowledge of the universal Spirit. But this cannot be achieved by the efforts of politicians, diplomats and administrators whose vision is warped by narrow considerations of personal, national and racial self-interest. The transformation can be brought about only by divinely inspired saints and sages who have experienced the universal vision of Truth or God, who are perfectly selfless and whose hearts are ever filled with love for all.

Love limited to one's country, loyalty confined to one's race, religion or community, attachment to one's family and identification of Self with one's body, are all alike the offsprings of ignorance which confine us in a cage of a smaller or bigger dimension. To fling one's life into the infinite expanse of the Divine is the work of heroes. Immortality is the birth-right of mankind.

The teachings of the ancient Rishis clearly show that ignorance of the one all-pervading Truth, whose nature is pure bliss, is the root-cause of fear, strife and misery. International conflicts, religious wrangles, social injustices, economic exploitations and political tyrannies are all found, in the ultimate analysis, to spring from selfishness born of the failure to realise the unity and universality of the Spirit. All World-Teachers unanimously declare: "O man! If you want peace for yourself and others in the world, adjust your conduct in accordance with the law of Love. Expand your vision so that it can embrace all fellow-beings and link them to yourself by Love. Rise above narrow creeds, cults, communal leanings and national ambitions. Merge your life in the infinity of God!"

Thus Speaks Ramdas, paras 108-112

Intuition is the Voice of God

The intellect is too feeble and limited to gauge the depths of the Infinite. It cannot find out the how and why of ignorance. Once we know we are caught in ignorance, our concern must only be to remove it, to get out of the cage, and not be enquiring into its cause and source. Sadhana is meant for breaking the walls of the cage.

Reason is a help, no doubt. It is surely a more reliable guide than the fickle mind. It helps us to discriminate between the Real and the unreal. But it helps only up to a limit. After a stage, it becomes a hindrance. It cannot be a safe guide throughout the spiritual journey. If you want to take leap into the Infinite and realise your oneness with It, you have to stop reasoning. Reason must give place to intuition. Intuition is born of a purified heart and an illumined intelligence. It is a spontaneous outflow of Divine Light. This can come only after the elimination of the ego-sense.

So long as intuition has not dawned in you, you have to be guided by reason. But reason is liable to go wrong. For, when reason works, the ego-sense is present. But when intuition is working, the ego-sense is absent. So intuition guides you unerringly. Intuition is the voice of God within you.

It is very hard for others to know whether, in a particular case, it is reason or intuition that is working in a person. It is a matter of inner experience for that person. Others cannot know it. But it is possible to a certain extent to find it out from what the person does or says. Perfect unselfishness is a mark of intuition. The intellect often works as an instrument of the ego. But it is difficult to know.

The intellect does not work by itself. It is acted on by the Self or Atman. The intellect can grasp external things. But it cannot turn back and grasp its own Divine Source. With a pair of tongs you can hold material objects. But the tongs cannot catch the hands which hold it. Similarly, the intellect cannot grasp God or Self—the higher Power behind it. The best use of the intellect is to help us know its own limitations.

Merely reading books on Vedanta and getting intellectually equipped with the ideas relating to the highest attainment cannot make one a true Vedantin. Learning is both a help and a hindrance. It is a hindrance if it feeds one's ego-sense and makes one pose as a person who has realised the Truth. God-realisation means experience of God. For this, humility is essential. Too much learning makes one proud. One must bend one's head to Him, realising the limitations of reason. It can take you only to the gate and it has to be left behind when you enter the realm of the Spirit. You haveto unlearn what you have learnt and become as simple and guileless as a child.

Modern philosophy begins with doubts about God and His existence. The ancient wisdom began with certitude. Westerners do not think with a purified intellect. So they are full of doubts. Their philosophy turns round in circles, without getting anywhere. They take dry intellectualism to be a sign of strength, and compassion in the heart to be weakness.

No amount of argument can make you understand the Truth. Direct perception and experience alone can grant you the vision of the Truth.

Thus Speaks Ramdas, paras 52-59

Japa: Oh! the Charm of the Name!

Take the Name as *Brahman* Himself and using it as a ladder ascend the summit, the supreme Godhead with whom you are eternally one.

The Divine Name is a powerful boat that takes man across the whirlpools of life to the haven of his eternal and spiritual nature. His Name transforms man from the human to the Divine. The Divine Name is the one sovereign panacea for all physical, mental, and intellectual ills that have created the sense of diversity and misery in the world.

To be in tune with the Name is to be in tune with the Infinite Truth and thus to transmute the lower, stumbling and ignorant human nature, into the glorious self-illumined nature.

The Divine Name purifies the mind of its ego and desires, and floods the whole being with light and joy.

Repeat the Name so constantly that its enthralling music should thrill, illumine, elevate and sweeten your entire life. The name arrests distracting thoughts, subdues unregulated desires and enlightens the intellect. After enabling its devotee to achieve thorough concentration of mind, it helps to draw the mind inward and attain complete absorption in the Eternal Reality, which in its turn takes him to the supreme goal of self-surrender.

The Name unlocks the fountain of your heart and floods your being with immortal light, knowledge, peace and joy. It grants you the loftiest vision and experience.

Fixing the mind on the sound of His Name is the easiest way for concentration. Take it that the sound of the Name is itself a symbol of God. By gradual practice, the external repetition will lead to an automatic functioning of the Name in the mind. When thus the Name comes into the mind constantly, you will attain concentration. By the Sadhana the restless nature of the mind is curbed.

Oh! the charm of the Name! It brings light where there is darkness, happiness where there is misery, contentment where there is dissatisfaction, bliss where there is pain, order where there is chaos, life where there is death, heaven where there is hell, God where there is Maya. He who takes refuge in that glorious Name knows no pain, no sorrow, no care, no misery. He lives in perfect Peace.

In all weathers cling to the Name of the Lord. It is the one plank which does not allow the man, who hangs on to it, to sink and be lost. The Name is the Lord, Guru and all in all.

When the Lord's Name is on our lips, we need not be afraid of anything in this world or in any other world. The Name is simple. It unveils layers of the deep-seated ignorance that had made you oblivious of your divine existence. It acts with a sure, steady and unfailing purpose. It is the real means for bringing about a complete state of self-surrender. Even from the start of the repetition of the Name, you begin to taste the nectar of immortality. As you go on, your joy increases and when this joy turns into ecstasy, it takes you beyond the body-idea and you become conscious of the Divine within you. Your individual sense disappears, as darkness in the presence of light. When this stage is reached a Sadhaka becomes a Siddha, i.e., the aspirant attains divine perfection.

The Name brings you self-absorption, and meditation becomes automatic, i.e., you are lost in the sweet rapture of the Spirit the moment you sit silent by yourself. The struggle the Sadhaka usually passes through, to keep the mind centred on the Truth, is not there for votary of the Name. He starts with joy, walks on the path with joy, and reaches the goal which is joy, and ultimately becomes Joy Itself. This is the sweetest consummation, all comprehensive perfection and the highest experience of the Godhead which the Name grants.

Mantra is a combination of words that stands for the Supreme Reality. It is so set that by the utterance of it a rhythmic sound is produced which has a marvellous effect on both the mental and the physical system. The sound of the Mantra produces mental equilibrium and physical harmony. It tunes the entire human being with the eternal music of the Divine. It lulls the feverishness of the mind. This equanimity in turn awakens the sleeping Divine Consciousness, bringing the soul in direct contact with the in-dwelling and all-pervading Reality. One great advantage of Mantra Yoga over other methods is that it is a discipline which is at once self-sufficient and independent. Truly, one who keeps the Mantra always on his lips can attain to the infinite power, wisdom, love and vision of God.

The Pathless Path, pp. 12-14

Japa: The Repetition of God's Name

The easiest means to make the mind dwell in the idea of God is to constantly reiterate mentally or vocally the Name of God. Such a recitation of the Name should of course be accompanied by implicit faith in the efficacy of the Name and intense love for the immortal ideal which the Name represents, viz. the supreme Reality who is absolute existence, consciousness and bliss and who is seated in the hearts of us all. When thus the mind is completely absorbed in the Divine idea, a stage is reached when the mere individual or physical consciousness is transmuted into the universal and ever blissful consciousness.

The Divine Life, p. 124

Question: *Is it advised that we should not do Japa as a stern and grim duty?*

Ramdas: What you say is true. Japa must be done with intense love and devotion for the object of your worship, that is, God. The Japa becomes spontaneous and gives you a rare joy as you go on doing it. You should not do it as a discipline imposed upon you by somebody else. If you do not get joy in doing Japa, you had better not do it, because it will not help you then. When you have love for God, Japa must give you great joy. Therefore, mystics say that repetition of God's name gives them ecstasy and they get a sweetness and joy which is indescribable. This shows that it is not mere mechanical repetition that helps us but a spontaneous outflow of our heart towards God in the repetition of His name. The object of repetition is to become conscious of the Divine presence within you and bring out the sweetness of your heart to the surface.

Ramdas Speaks, vol. 2, pp. 126-127

Japam Purifies the Mind

He who has unshakable faith in the Name is saved.

In all weathers cling to the name of the Lord. It is the one plank which does not allow the man, who hangs on to it, to sink and be lost. The Name is the Lord, the Guru, and all in all.

Japam purifies the mind, and enables the aspirant to attain the knowledge of Truth.

Weakness is felt only when God is forgotten. And the simple way to remember Him is to take His Name constantly.

Let us cling to His glorious Name with all love and faith, and let Him do what He pleases with us. Ours is to realise our immortality.

Let the whole life be lived out as an offering to Him who has brought us into being. Let His Name be ever on our lips and in our minds.

Repetition of the holy Mantram purifies the mind. Satsang elevates you and grants you right knowledge. Last comes Gurukripa. The awareness of it makes you realise that you are the embodiment of an eternal existence full of bliss and peace.

Constant repetition of Ram-mantram and practice of meditation will give you the needed strength and courage to overcome all weaknesses of the mind and the heart.

Repetition of the Ram-mantram, meditation on the attributes of God and surrender of all your actions to the Lord, form the way.

When the Lord's Name is on our lips we need not be afraid in this world or in any other world. Do not forget that you are the immortal Truth.

A heart that wells up with love is the very heart of God. God is Nirguna but He is also Saguna as pure, spontaneous, universal love. We can tune ourselves to this love through the melodious music of His Name.

The easiest method by which we can keep God-remembrance is repetition of His glorious Name. Be always cheerful, fearless and free.

The divine Name is the one refuge for the man struggling for the Darshan of God.

Indeed, the power of God's Name is simply marvellous. It can take man to the highest and the loftiest Truth of world existence. The Name grants him a state of unalterable freedom, bliss and peace.

Direct your vision inward and realise the glory of the Atman. The key that unlocks the door to this spiritual kingdom within you is Ramnam.

You may call Him by any name you like, but the Truth is always one and the same.

The Sayings of Ramdas, pp. 19-21

Jesus is an Incarnation of Infinite Love

Jesus Christ is an incarnation of infinite Love. He is a beacon light in the shoals and storms of life. To be inspired by his Spirit is to transmute life into an illumined expression of God. The very thought of Christ brings peace and purity to the mind. How blessed does indeed life become when the mind ever dwells in him. The secret of realisation of a great ideal is to become the ideal itself by ceaseless thought and meditation of it, so much so, that the individual becomes the very form and image of the ideal by self-absorption and self-surrender. Thereafter, life is lived in the vision and glory of the ideal.

What is the importance of the cross on which Christ was crucified? Cross is an eternal symbol of a supreme sacrifice. For the salvation of the world, stricken with ignorance, Christ laid down his precious life. A greater sacrifice could not have been made by one who came to save the world.

Visualise the heart of Christ for a moment. How sublime it is! It is pure gold ever shining with the lustre of compassion, forgiveness and peace. It is a heart that thrills in symphony with the ailing heart of mankind. The waves of love that go out of it seek to soothe, heal and purify the heart of every being.

Christ's vision—how unbounded and infinite it is! It embraces all beings and creatures, nay, it envelops the entire Universe. It is a vision born of a consciousness of unity of all life and manifestation—it fulfils itself in universal Love.

Christ's words—how simple and direct but at the same time how sweetened with the honey of love and kindness! His words ever convey the message of love, sacrifice and goodwill. "Love one another" is the keynote of his teachings. Through this love alone he taught that man can inherit the kingdom of bliss, peace and immortality.

Christ held—Faith in God is not a fetish—is not a sign of one who belongs to a particular organisation or school of thought. The man of true faith serves his fellowmen through his love of the eternal, i.e. God, who dwells equally in his own heart and in the hearts of all beings. The humble servant of humanity is the true servant of God.

The glory of his message is revealed in these words: "This is my command, that ye love one another, even as I have loved you."

O Christ—Let thy Love-universal prevail in the world and dispel the grim clouds of strife and war that are gathering over it. Let thy goodwill and mercy remove the discordant notes prevailing everywhere.

Christ is not merely a body as many of us believe. He is a symbol of cosmic Reality as all great Teachers are. He is an expression of the supreme Spirit. To reach him, to be inspired by him and to be guided by him is to be identified with him in Spirit. It is in the pure heart that he reveals himself. May Christ—the divine Spirit—pour his grace on the world and quell the fires of destruction that are raging in it! May his love prevail in the hearts of warring nations!

The Divine Life, pp. 183-184, 187

Joy is His Nature

Among a certain class of spiritual aspirants it is a belief that religion is associated intimately with a sad and melancholy attitude, that the sign of true devotion is a long face, sagging lips, knitted forehead, lowered eyebrows and such other manifestations of a deep-seated sorrow. There are, no doubt, moments in the life of the aspirant when his mind sinks into a state of dejection, and sometimes of despair. But such shadows and darkness pass away, giving place to brightness and sunshine. The struggle of an aspirant is heroic in nature. With the aid of prayers and continuous remembrance of God, he battles against the tendencies of his lower nature, which throw obstacles in his path. The mere fact that he is going to meet his supreme Beloved grants him the needed strength and cheer in his endeavour to approach Him. Whenever he meets with failures, he gets over the reaction produced by them on him, by resigning himself to the will of God. Resignation to His will means the release of a divine force, hidden so long in him, which infuses strength and courage into his mind, heart and soul. So the outlook of the true aspirant is optimistic. His eyes see only beauty, goodness and love everywhere. In every happening he discerns the seed of hope and achievement. In this way, he conquers the moods of depression that seek to subdue him. Satva Guna, or the quality of light and harmony, is the prominent feature of his life. His face is bright and cheerful. He takes life and all that it brings for him, not seriously.

His heart is light. He enjoys a joke and gives himself away to a hearty laugh. After he has met his Beloved, his joy knows no bounds. He lives in perennial ecstasy. He is frank and playful like a child, and creates a jovial atmosphere wherever he is. People who come in touch with him therefore become, like him, free and blissful. God is not a god of sadness, but He is rightly defined by sages and saints, who have realised Him, as *Sat-Chit-Anand*—absolute existence, consciousness and *bliss.* Joy is His nature. To strive to reach Him is joy. Every step we put forward in our progress towards Him is joy. To think of him is joy. Even to feel sometimes separate from Him is also joy. All through the thoughts, words and acts, should run an unbroken stream of His remembrance, and this is supreme joy. When you at last reach His feet, and lose yourself in His glorious being, you yourself become joy. Then, where is the place for sorrow, suffering and melancholy? Ramdas would have the aspirant walk the divine path with a nimble step, joy in his heart, cheer and smile on the face, singing sweetly His enchanting name, all the way calling Him as Mother, heart overflowing with love for Him. In this manner, go and have Her Darshan, and be blessed for ever!

The Divine Life, pp. 41-42

Life Has a Beautiful Meaning and Purpose

What is required to set life free and make it blessed is to do all actions in the spirit of perfect surrender to the will of the all-wise Master—the master of your being and of the world-existence. This is possible in all the fields of activity in which you are placed in consonance with your nature and attainments.

Life is a game with which you play as you play with a doll. All the emotions and passions you exhibit in this play are the necessary and inevitable movements of it. When you observe, as an unaffected witness, this most wonderful game of life made up of the clash of ideals, interests and thoughts, you realise that it is there before you only as a sport and nothing else. The goal which Ramdas places before all people is nothing short of an independence and freedom, born of the submission to the Divine Power which controls, guides and actuates every individual in the course of his or her life on this earth. To live like "dumb-driven cattle" is not the purpose of life. Each individual has to draw upon all the latent resources of his or her existence in order to rise to the height of absolute freedom—a freedom by virtue of which he or she yields, wherever it is necessary to yield, and stands firm like a rock, wherever it is proper to do so. To be a timid creature without firm convictions, vacillating at every passing breeze and circumstance, is indeed to become an object of pity on the part of some and of derision on the part of others.

"Success and failure be the same to you", is a truism to be realised in order to attain a peaceful mind. Whatever God determines should be implicitly believed as for the best. Really, every loss, failure and misfortune is pregnant with absolute good. It must be recognised with full faith that, at the back of the relative mind, exists a Divinity which causes all its workings—a Divinity which is the very abode of peace and bliss.

Success in life depends upon a daring and determined course taken up through unshakable faith and confidence. Vacillation is the greatest handicap to success. By taking complete refuge in the Almighty, you should decide upon a definite line of action, and then, by an unflinching perseverance, carry it out through good or ill. When taking such a step, do not rely for help and guidance from any body in the world except upon your Self. God—the great Self in you—is your help and guide in all matters. In accordance with His command pursue any path which He prompts you to. All power, strength and wisdom are within you, because the great Self who is all these is your true being. He will see that your life is a magnificent success. Harbour no doubts or misgivings. Faith and grit win the race. Strengthen your will by surrender to the Divine Will. Turn your mind within for divine peace. Rouse yourself in every way and bravely fight this battle of life, which is a battle for all alike, and come out triumphant as a soldier of love and peace and goodwill.

Life is a perpetual adjustment and readjustment—it is an ever changing movement on the surface—but in its depths it is perfect calmness, peace and stillness. Since universal motion is a wave from the infinite silence and repose, it has the nature of the source from which it has sprung. So, bliss is the beginning, the middle and the end of all things—be it static or dynamic.

Really, human life becomes blessed when God brings about occasions for turning its course towards Himself. Thereafter God takes up such a life and guides and controls it according to His supreme will, which works always for good.

Life, in every condition can be lived in freedom and joy, provided the soul within remains unattached to external forms of life.

When the flow of life becomes spontaneous, it is always surcharged with the glory of pure love and service. What a splendid gift is human life!

The man who does not behold the finger of God working all events and happenings experiences needless suffering. Therefore, peace and contentment belong only to those who have submitted, in all the vicissitudes of life, to the supreme will of God.

Instead of allowing your mind to externalise itself, do make it go inward and mingle and merge in the depths of your being, where dwell ever-lasting life, peace and joy.

To behold the Truth within oneself, and then in all beings and creatures alike, is the true vision of life. The purpose and goal of life is to realise your immortality and the eternal union and identity with the supreme Beloved who is the immanent and transcendent Lord of the Universe.

The object of your life is to be happy yourself and give happiness to others. In fact, real delight consists in so adjusting your life as to make it yield joy to others. If you have faith in God, use this faith in cultivating patience and equanimity. Faith always goes with cheerfulness, resignation and peace. Be childlike—not childish—be blissful and a free child of God. Reveal your innate divine nature, and diffuse around you always love and joy.

By struggle you conquer. Struggle means development of will-power and a gradual awakening to the real purpose of life—which is Self-realisation. Make every influence on your life, favourable or unfavourable, work for your spiritual advancement. Give up controversy, discussion and justification, by subduing sensitiveness and sentiment. God's name is your help. Feel less and less the so-called heavy responsibilities of life which you have imposed on yourself. The truth is, the moment you are free from attachment and sense of possession, the whole world is at your feet. Have no misgivings, throw overboard world's opinion. Rise above these petty things. Be tremendously earnest and determined in your spiritual quest.

Surely life has a beautiful meaning and purpose when it is understood to be of an universal nature and significance. The utmost grandeur of it is revealed when it breaks through every sense of division and diversity, and sheds all around soothing light of pure, spontaneous love—the rapture of an inexplicable joy and peace.

Every power with which you are gifted has to be cheerfully utilised for the service of God in the world. It is also the experience of every great soul, who has dedicated his or her life for relieving the distress of the world, that the path is one of acute suffering. Hence self-sacrifice has been the badge of saints all over the world. The lamp can give light only at the cost of its oil. "Give and give", is the law of the deathless spirit working in nature. The whole beauty of life lies in its utter dedication.

This life is not worth living if it is not consecrated to the devotion of Sri Ram—if it is not offered up completely to His service. For attaining this you have to cry to Him day and night for His grace. Yes, Ram is very kind. He is ever ready to fulfil the wishes of His humble devotees. You have only to pray to Him to enable you to keep up His remembrance continuously, ceaselessly. Don't ask for anything else. "I pray to you, Oh! Love Infinite, for only this—Your remembrance, which means Your Darshan."

An active life is perfectly in keeping with Self-realisation and divine service. What is needed is a total dedication of your entire life to Him. In all situations maintain a steady consciousness of Divinity within and about you. Do not harass your mind with thoughts of weakness. Infinite strength is within you. Drawing inspiration and power from this source, be cheerful and contented at all times. Let the name of the Lord dwell ever in your mind!

From whatsoever angle, Ramdas looks at the world, he finds nothing wrong anywhere. Everything is as it should be. Because one Truth pervades everywhere—one life has revealed itself in infinite forms. So you are all children of that Truth—that Life—nay you are yourself the Truth—the Life.

Some people prefer to call themselves sinners. They must be wishing to enjoy the fun of it. Else, what to make of the way they speak of themselves? They are offering a direct insult to God when they dub themselves sinners. This is as good as denying His very existence. If you believe that He is, you would not care to know whether you are a monument of virtue or mountain of iniquity. You would only feel that you are simply as God made you. You have a harp which is ever tuned to one strain. It sings only of sin, misery and death. Do change the song to one of peace, joy and immortality.

Your life has to be lived not for yourself, but for the sake of all those with whom God has ordained you should come in contact from time to time. The purpose of life is to take delight in giving peace and joy to others. This you can do in every circumstance and condition of life. Life means service. The true joy of service is felt only when you make it a spontaneous flow from the fountain of your immortal existence. Hence, self-surrender has been held forth as the means for the realisation of your immortal nature and the consequent blissful activity.

Whatever circumstances you may find yourself in, do not forget the great and merciful Lord of the universe. Life bereft of the thought of God is verily not worth living. God is our mother, guide and protector. To be in constant awareness of Him means purity, strength, courage and peace; because God is all power, knowledge and bliss.

The world is a world at all times. The playful nature of it in which every kind of creature and event exists is as it should be. What is needed is a change within you, by which you open your true sight, and look upon the world as a Lila of the Lord. This state is attained by merging your relative existence into God's absolute being. Ceaseless remembrance of the Lord is the way.

Glimpses of Divine Vision, pp. 1-14

Life is Intended for Attaining This Supreme Goal

It is up to you to make your life either harmonious or chaotic. If you attune it with God, the Master of harmonies, and make Him your sole Companion, Guide and Refuge, you will fill it with true beauty, peace and equality. Then, eternal music is produced in you and divine splendour illumines every aspect of your life. On the contrary, if your life is ruled and controlled by egoism, all the forces within you, mental and physical, will create a state of discord and confusion.

The way is to so adjust your life and conduct as to harmonize it with the cosmic life and activity, which means that you become one with all beings and creatures by developing universal love and vision. Your life is now surcharged with the glory, power and peace divine.

Your individual life should be realised as the expression of the universal life. It must bear the stamp of God upon it. The animal and even the human in you should be totally transformed into the divine life and nature. You have to become the embodiment of immortal love and joy.

Life is intended for attaining this supreme goal. If you choose to remain only in your lower, dark and egoistic nature, you will be a victim to unbridled passions and live in bondage and misery. Therefore, reveal your divinity and make life blessed.

Let not false aspirations arise in your heart and low desires dominate you. Have God, the King of your heart, as your sole inspirer. He is not far away. He dwells within you. Be aware of Him and surrender up your entire being unto Him. You feel His presence within you when your heart is pure, your mind is enlightened and your will coalesces with His will.

When you are thus possessed by the Divine Spirit, you are imbued with His radiance and power for bringing about an atmosphere of peace and goodwill on the earth and for removing all causes that give rise to strife, conflict and war. The fragrance of divine love which now emanates from you is irresistible. You will sweeten your own life and also the lives of others. Your vision is sublime, as it beholds only Divinity everywhere. The kindly and soothing light of your eyes kindles other hearts and awakens them to the consciousness of God. They are thus made lights unto themselves and lights to all the world.

The world is passing through a period of great travail and agony. They are the signs of a new birth which will bring goodwill, peace and harmony on earth. Let us all be the heralds of this great event. May divine grace pour on the world and cool down the fires of greed and hate, the cause of destructive wars and the resultant widespread devastation, distress and death.

The Divine Life, pp. 33-34

Life Lived in the Thought of God

Life is short. Make the most of it by living in God. Everyday that passes brings you nearer to the end, when you shall have to depart from the world leaving behind everything which you hugged as your own. Life lived in the thought of God is a life lived in true joy and peace. Else it is a lengthening chain of woe that drags you ultimately to the terrifying jaws of death.

Human life is solely intended for the enjoyment of eternal bliss. If, on the other hand, a man makes it a hot-bed of cares, anxieties, fears and doubts, he would only be wasting a rare and precious gift which God has granted him.

Man's greatness lies not
In fading laurels won
In earthly riches gained
In days of wanton revelry.
Man can rise above man
To everlasting glory
To deathless beatitude
To immortal Life and Joy.

The object of human life is to realise the joy and peace of the indwelling God.

Man's quest for happiness can end only by his realising the fountain of Eternal Joy residing within himself.

Human life is a magnificent gift of God. Raise it beyond the range of mental conceptions and cogitations. Lift it beyond the relative, conditioned and fettered entanglements of the ever changing phenomenal life so that it might know itself as the ever free, ever blissful and ever existing Reality.

The upward flight of the soul is always towards its perfect identity with the Great One who is the same through and in all. The river of life struggles through all obstacles and conditions to reach the vast and infinite ocean of existence,—God. It knows no rest, no freedom and no peace until it mingles with the waters of immortality and delights in the vision of infinity.

The Pathless Path, pp. 1-2

Love Begets Love

Love begets love. Love is life, love is Truth. The highest attainment is love, the loftiest goal is love.

The cosmic vision held out in the *Gita* alone can enable you to attain universal love. This vision or love grants you neverfading joy and peace. To love God is to love all, and to love all is to love God. This is the secret of Self-realisation and liberation, and Ram-nam is the way.

Indeed every movement of your mind in thought, every movement of your tongue in words, every movement of your limbs in activity or works, is the play of Shakti. Shakti is nothing but God's love. When we realise that all movement is the movement of that supreme love, we live continuously in a state of divine ecstasy which is simply inexpressible. The, Prem fills us through and through, in other words, we are soaked in Prem. The quality of Prem is Anand. There is also the witness of this play of love or Shakti—the immutable, changeless, all-pervading, static aspect of your being, whose quality is ineffable peace: On this unaffected screen of eternal peace dances, in flitting forms, infinite love producing sweet intoxicating music of Anand. Every particle of your body and the whole universe is thrilling with Sri Ram's love. So, there is nothing but Anand in all movement, change and activity. There is nothing but peace in the depths of all forms—result of movement and change. So, eternal peace and bliss are the only Reality.

Everybody wants to eat only sweet things. The thought of bitter things is repulsive to all. Love—pure and glorious love—the immortal divine love—makes us drink always sweetness and joy. Therefore, to open your hearts to the inflow of this intoxicating love and remain ever in the rapture of it is the supreme blessing and purpose of life. All things pass away—your petty ambitions and unregulated aspirations are things of the moment. Your pleasures and pains, your successes and failures, your exultations and depressions, and your desires and fancies, all, all pass away. The one thing that remains unaltered, permanent and eternal is Divine Love.

Love does not rest content with merely loving, but flows out in acts of service. Love is blissful only when it freely gives itself away. Therefore, it is truly said—"The giver and the receiver are both blessed."

Love must ever be revealed in service; otherwise, love has no value, or love is no love. Love cheerfully sacrifices; love willingly suffers. Where such love is, there is real peace and joy. Such a love illumines and blesses life.

O Love! There is nothing greater than Thee! Love is Truth. Love is God. Love is all. The name of this love is Ram. So, to repeat this name is to realise this supreme Love—is to enjoy everlasting bliss.

Glimpses of Divine Vision, pp. 49-53

Love Breaks All Barriers

Divine Love is the highest attainment. All spiritual practices should end in this sweet consummation. Love is the end of the quest. See that you are absorbed in God who is Love and become an image of Him. Let all your emotions be of love. Life is dry and insipid if it is not filled with love. Be intoxicated with love—the love that blesses you with a vision of your Beloved. All beings are the forms of your Beloved. Grace, Love and Bliss are synonymous. The three are one in your Beloved and you are He. Dance with joy!

The victories of the intellect and the highest flights of imagination, cannot be compared with the triumphs of love. The discords and conflicts in life are the result of the absence of love. Love purifies, ennobles and sanctifies every movement of life. Love invites sufferings for the sake of the Beloved and transmutes them into unalloyed joy. The pointed dart tipped with love injects delight, not pain.

Ordinary love based on physical affinity is a source of misery both to the lover and the loved. But Divine Love based on the feeling of spiritual oneness is sublime. It is a source of pure bliss. Here you love another not because he is a relation of yours, but because you and he are one in Spirit.

Love in the making sees faults; love in the fulfilment sees none. Seeing faults is like cutting love into pieces, murdering love. By so doing we keep the mind alive. We have to go beyond the mind. The mind must die.

Love breaks all barriers. Even body-consciousness is transcended under the intoxication of love. What to say then of man-made distinctions created by allegiance to creed, race, and institutions? Love is a great unifying force. It is a solvent of differences and diversities. It creates unity. But to love truly, one must have knowledge of the Self. On the basis of Self-knowledge alone one can love all with an equal eye.

Love begets love and kindness begets kindness. This is a law which knows no exception. People dislike us because we have no love for them. If we love them, their love automatically flows to us. When our love goes to them and their love comes to us, the two streams mingle together and there is an ocean of love and joy. Love is not bargaining; it is not give and take. It is a spontaneous merging of souls.

Truly speaking, it is not that we have to love God; we have to know that God who is Love is enthroned in our hearts. By surrendering ourselves to this Divine Love in us, we become embodiments of that Love. By constant remembrance and meditation we realise His presence in us and our life becomes filled with His light and love. His love then radiates through us and we see with love, talk with love, give with love, receive with love and act with love.

Love of God means love of all beings, because God is all and all is in God. He is all in all. Love is consciousness of unity as hatred is of diversity. Go beyond all narrow limitations. Rise, soar high and hold the world in one embrace of Love. Your dwelling place is the whole universe which is your body. Live in it as Love!

Thus Speaks Ramdas, paras 80-87

Love is the Expression of God

Love is the expression of God. To realise love is to realise God. God is all-pervading and is seated in the hearts of all beings, creatures and things. To love all it to be in tune with God, i.e. to become conscious of our perfect oneness with every form of manifestation in the universe. The first thing necessary for a man to attain this all-absorbing and glorious love is that he should be freed from the baneful clutches of lust, greed and wrath, because these passions, taking their stand upon the separative ego-sense, throw a cloud or veil over this self-luminous, self-existent and immortal source of love within him. The eradication of the ego with its dark movements can be possible, by a continuous meditation of the indwelling Reality or God and by a process of surrender of all actions to the same Lord, who causes all activity and movements in the worlds. Action thus done in the gradual sublimation of the ego-sense expands the vision and purifies the mind, enabling it to find union with the all-blissful Truth or God.

The path of self-surrender declared in the sublime teachings of the *Gita* is the easiest one, and this fact is borne witness to by the galaxy of sages and saints, both of the past and the present ages. Krishna, Mohammed, Buddha and Jesus Christ—founders of the four great religions of the world—perfectly agree in that they point to this path alone as the supreme way to the attainment of God, i.e. immortality and peace.

Compassion, forgiveness and peace are the conditions governing self-surrender. Love denotes a combination of these triple virtues. To surrender to God is to be God-like or to be God Himself. God is all compassion, mercy and goodness. Hence to acquire these qualities by self-purification and self-surrender, is to approach God and ultimately become one with Him.

The aspirant who longs to realise the blessedness of his union with God must become perfectly harmless in thought, word and deed. His heart must well up with love for all beings and creatures without regard to any distinction; and he must also possess an equal or universal vision. The aspirant should be guided not only by the noble principle of not returning evil for evil in any manner, but also by a still higher principle of returning good for evil. Thus forgiveness and mercy are held forth as the great attributes, essentially to be cultivated by the earnest seeker according to the teachings of all incarnations, saints and sages of the world.

It is better for him, thinks the aspirant, to die in the practice of forgiveness rather than live through revenge, because while one elevates him to the immortal status, the other drags him further deep into the hell of ever-recurring births and deaths. Indeed a death, in whatever form it comes, when his soul rests on the bosom of the Infinite and when he has no ill will, hate or enmity towards any living creature on the face of the earth, could be welcomed with cheerfulness and resignation. This is the cult of Christ and Buddha. Krishna and Mohammed show by their life and teachings that the other extreme way is also possible under the same spiritual condition of the aspirant. Surrender grants him not only the knowledge that he is the immortal spirit, but also that he is in all his physical activities a mere instrument in the hands of the Almighty. In this state of liberation or self-surrender, God could use him as an instrument to destroy without hatred—for the existence of which the ego-sense is responsible—and which is now absent, the evil forces that work against the progressive march of humanity to the great purpose of God, viz. the establishment of harmony, goodwill and peace in the world.

When all the peoples are united in the spirit, through mutual love and toleration under the banner of the one supreme Lord dwelling in the hearts of them all, they attain to a power which bestows nothing but pure peace, freedom and joy. The people who stand for distinctions and divisions not only suffer untold miseries as a result of them, but also raise the instruments of God for their own destruction.

So, O ye people of the world, unite in the freedom of your immortal existence for enjoying the pure bliss through universal love, by acts of self-sacrifice, sympathy, compassion and forgiveness. Do not be any longer caught by the external forms and formalities, customs and traditions and dogmas and rituals that should disappear or change with the passing of time. Persistence in these non-essentials has given rise to the present state of chaos and confusion, since they obstruct the free play of the undercurrent of love upon which is founded the real unity and peace of the world. Stand together as children of the same parent in the radiance of the Almighty Lord of the universe who is at once immanent and transcendent, and enjoy the supreme blessings of true peace and freedom.

The Divine Life, pp. 134-136

Love is the Mystic Solvent of All Diversity

God is defined as Love. What does this word Love here signify? What is its real nature? Love is absolute and is perfectly impersonal; it is the pure and dazzling power of the Spirit that dwells in and pervades all beings and things. Love is infinite and eternal. Love is beyond the implications of name and form—still it works through them. Love is beyond the sense of duality—still it reveals in multifarious ways. It is the omnipotent power that guides and controls all things.

Love is unaffected by the touch of time and place. The so-called right and wrong are unknown in the realm of Love. It is not coloured by the conflict of opposites and the modes of nature. Its light is of a crystal. Love is spontaneous in expression and therefore supremely blissful. Its manifestation is based upon its indivisible unity and oneness with all that exists. Love is the one truth and one power. Love is ever taintless, ever flowing and ever acting from a transcendent plane. The upward movement and the downward both belong to Love. All opposites neutralise in the undifferentiated spirit of Love. Love is the mystic solvent of all diversity.

To realise God who is Love, you are asked to love one another; to look upon others in the same light as yourself; to feel for others as you do for yourself. Can you understand the secret of this Love if you only strive to attain it through physical or mental perfection without seeking for a greater ideal? No, this is not possible. On no lower plane can you love another as yourself. You have to transcend individuality; you have to rise higher than the body and mind and realise the universal and immutable essence of your being, and then alone can you love another as yourself—not otherwise. You must attain to that consciousness in which you experience the ecstasy of oneness with all beings and creatures in the world. You must feel at the core of your heart that you, another and all are forms of one underlying Spirit. Diversity is merely on the surface. In the splendour of Truth, you and all are one.

In the vision of oneness and sameness of the life-principle there can be no dualism and the consequent clash of opposites. This vision is of Love—a pure emanation of an almighty and impersonal Spirit. Love's nature is therefore equality and harmony founded on the knowledge of oneness of all beings.

Compassion is the first quality to be developed in order to attain the bliss of impersonal Love. At the sight of suffering your heart is touched and it melts. In a mysterious way you now feel the suffering of another as your own. This feeling is not of the body or mere mind. It is the outcome of a consciousness of something that equally dwells within you and the sufferer, and which is undivided. By a strange impulse you are urged to succour him Your act of relief, whatever shape it takes, yields you inexplicable peace and joy. Verily, the peace that you thus derive has sprung from nowhere but the outer fulfilment of your intuitive or mystic realisation of inner identity with the sufferer. When impelled on by Love, you invariably take your stand on the impersonal truth of your existence.

So long as you are only seeking for perfection of Love in the relative good conceived by you as an ideal, you will be caught in the labyrinth of a never-ending quest. Understand at once that the root of Love is in your impersonal Self and to realise it, awakening the heart to the feeling of compassion and the resultant selfless action is essential. Perform life's all activities in such a manner that you can every moment be conscious of your identity with the whole creation. Do not rely on any standard, however exalted, which is merely dogmatic, ethical or mental. Soar beyond all conditioned states of thought and life, and, reaching the infinite Reality, make this great Impersonal as the one immortal standard of your entire life. This Truth or God has become all—there is none besides He.

The Divine Life, pp. 142-144

Man is an Embodied Divinity

Human life has a great purpose behind it. It is not given to be lived out in ignorance of the divine source from which it springs. When the source is known it flows like a sparkling stream imbued with immortal joy and peace, diffusing its beneficence for all alike. Otherwise, life assumes a dull and monotonous aspect—fitful, erratic and disturbed. It loses its inherent tranquillity and bliss. It is covered by a dark shadow. It feels that it is fettered by innumerable ties. It is like a bird trapped in a cage and struggling for freedom.

True freedom, peace and joy can come only when life realises its universal, eternal and infinite nature. It is the dissolution of the individual ego in the cosmic consciousness—God. It is filling life with divine love and splendour.

It is now that life reveals the glory of God's own power. It becomes a veritable expression of it. Therefore it is able to control and guide all other forces in nature. It should not be mistaken that life at a standstill is the true life. Such a life can be compared to a stagnant pool. It is self-centred, self-satisfied and therefore moves in a narrow circle and can never taste the peace of immortality. As the fragrance rises from the incense, as the lustre radiates from a diamond, as the perfume spreads from a flower, so life should manifest its hidden beauty, power, light and joy.

Man is an embodied divinity. He can raise himself to the heights of spiritual eminence. He can experience his absolute and deathless existence. He can make every atom of his manifest life thrill with the divine consciousness. He can know his oneness with the visible nature and invisible worlds. Apparently an individual—still he lives and acts ever in tune with the Infinite.

So let your wisdom be of the Eternal, your love be of the Infinite and your actions bear the stamp of universality. Thus realise the supreme perfection of your life. Verily, you are He.

The Divine Life, pp. 34-35

Meditation: Posture and Method for Silent Meditation

Mind is a veil that shuts you from the splendour of your immortal spirit, which is your real being. Tear up this veil by means of constant meditation and self-surrender. Retire within yourself from time to time and lose your little ego in the infinite consciousness of your supreme self. You are verily the embodiment of truth. Wake up to this awareness.

Concentration

What is needed for the beginner is to arrest the restless nature of the mind, a steady practice at concentration. To achieve this end, Ramdas found the constant repetition of the Guru-Mantram as a sovereign means. The wandering mind is thus brought under control and is fixed at one point.

This point is God—the symbol and spirit of the Mantram.

Meditation

Side by side with the repetition of the Mantram bring into the mind the glorious attributes of God. "God is within me—God is Infinite—God is Bliss, Purity and Peace—God is Light of Lights and the Power of Powers—God is the Master of Worlds—God is the Doer and the Non-Doer at once—God is Knowledge, Love, Compassion and Forgiveness—God is the one Truth and one Reality—The Universe is God's Self-revelation—God dwells in all beings, creatures and things—God fills all spheres and planes of life—My body, mind, senses and intellect and soul are all God's—God permeates my being—I am God's very image—both as the Revealed and unrevealed—There exists nothing but God—God is all in all—GOD IS ALL."

Meditation is nothing but a method of autosuggestion. The veil of ignorance which is an obsession can be removed only by a continued hammering on the mind, of the Immortal nature of your true being. Successful meditation requires a well-controlled and concentrated mind, for which the following rules have to be observed:

1. Diet, Satwic food, i.e. Non-irritant foods.
2. Solitude.
3. Society of saints.
4. Devotional music.
5. Reading the lives and teachings of saints.

Posture and Method for Silent Meditation

1. Sit up in any steady Asana suitable for you with your spinal cord and head erect.

2. Shut your eyes but internally direct your gaze between the eye-brows and gradually to the crown of the head. Sit fixed in this gaze.

3. Repeat the Mantram mentally for some time to stop the wavering mind.

4. Then when the mind is calmed down, mentally repeat the great attributes of God one by one.

5. This process repeated from day to day will bring on self-absorption giving you the vision of lights, etc.

6. Go still deeper into the realm of utter silence and stillness of your higher self or spirit, and rise completely above the body. Now you will realise the undifferentiated aspect of God bringing on the experience of your absolute identity with God.

7. Come out of this state—which would be difficult in the

beginning but can be possible by the exercise of a strong will and for you the world outside will now stand transformed as the very expression or manifestation of God—everywhere the Light of God will dazzle your eyes; even in the apparent diversity and activity of nature you will strangely be conscious of an all-pervading stillness and peace of the Eternal—a consciousness which is unshakably permanent.

You will also feel that you are liberated from the harassing dualities of life followed by the crowning experience of an abiding state of ineffable ecstasy.

Ineffable Ecstasy

The ineffable bliss experienced when the individual sense is dissolved in the Supreme Consciousness of God is the highest acquisition of human life. When the source of immortal joy is opened within us, it flows and saturates every fibre of our being, internal and external, and makes our life at once a waveless peace and ceaseless thrill of ecstasy. Death, fear, and grief have then no significance for us. You see and feel a round of joy and delight in all movements, in the visible expressions of the undivided and eternal life and Truth. The one splendour of Divine light envelops and pervades all forms and things; the one VISION OF ENDLESS PEACE AND BLISS dazzles and enchants you everywhere. Nay, you realise that you and the Universe are form and substance of the Infinite Truth. Oh! the sublimity of this exalted state—indescribable state—blessed indeed are those who are filled with this inexhaustible nectar of Immortality.

The Pathless Path, pp. 23-26

Mohammed: The Great Prophet

From the sandy deserts of Arabia a heavenly light arose—the very light of God. At a time when Arabia was the hotbed of internecine wars and the people were steeped in superstition, and the wail of the poor and the helpless was rending the air, the great Prophet Mohammed came.

The Prophet bore in his hand the blazing torch of a Divine message from the Almighty—a message of peace, unity and brotherhood for all humanity. His heart melted with compassion at the miserable state of things around him.

He weaned away the ill-directed thought and aspiration of the uncontrolled and ignorant masses, and turned their vision towards the Almighty Creator of the worlds. His powerful personality, inspired with the spirit of God, dominated over the Arabs and, subduing the evils of selfishness, greed and violence, established in their hearts a healing and ennobling faith in the all-merciful Lord.

Thus the great Prophet brought peace and a close-knitting feeling of brotherhood amongst a discontented and divided people. Through incessant exhortations, coupled with his exalted touch and transforming influence, he softened their heart and filled it with the pure emotions of compassion, love and sympathy. He taught them the principle of prayer, by which the heart could be raised to approach the throne of God.

The Prophet resolutely stood for God, unity and peace. He laid great stress upon the all-peaceful and all-merciful nature of

God, and held that surrender to His will is the path to attain everlasting life and beatitude.

The Prophet's vision is distinctly universal. He realised the entire humanity as a united whole and revealed to man the mystery of his intimate relationship with God—the Divine Originator. Verily, real harmony and the resultant peace and goodwill can be possible when all mankind come to recognise the suzerainty of the Godhead and live on this blessed earth, in a spirit of friendliness and co-operation beneath the banner of Hill all-powerful and holy Name. God is the one supreme cause and the one compassionate Parent of all that exists. The Prophet's message, as it is inspired by God, is a message for all peoples of this planet.

The Divine Life, pp. 178-179

Mysticism in Excelsis

God is an artist *par excellence*. He has painted the picturesque universe on the screen of His own immutable and glowing Spirit. So He is at once the painter and the painted. In the ultimate analysis, God and His lover, God and His devotee and servant, are He. The unmanifest—which is beyond all duality has become both. This secret few know.

Discrimination, which is the power granted by God to distinguish the real from the unreal, awoke me. This is the Grace that worked from within. Then the Grace came from without—the Grace from the Guru—which completed the circuit, as it were. Sadhana done to bring about this contact resulted in a flood of illumination. Now the aspirant is lost in God—in divine rapture and peace.

God is Love, Knowledge and Power. He made me realise Him first as Love, then as Knowledge and last as Power. Now my life entire is fulfilled in Him, so much so that my life has become His life and being. I am conscious that I am one with Him and all the worlds, beings and things, because He is all and all in all.

We speak too much about God, remaining in the plane of duality. Let identity with Him in Spirit be the basis for all that we say and do. We cannot have full satisfaction in mere dualism—as two entities, God and I. Twoness in play is all right.

There is the peril of discarding all duality as utter illusion and striving for liberation in non-duality, taking it as the only nature of the Reality. No, if that were so, life in the field of manifestation has not any sense or meaning. It will then be only a phantasmagoria—grotesque and chaotic. On the other hand, it is a play or Lila full of significance—a beautiful and enchanting image or picture of God.

Oh God! How good and great Thou art. Thou art my Mother and I am Thy child. I play on Thy lap knowing that mother and child, in the rapture of Love—union, are ever one. This is mysticism *in excelsis.*

The Divine Life, pp. 207-208

Nanak: The Founder of the Sikh Religion

A brilliant prophet of Truth made his appearance, on the horizon of the Punjab, in the middle of the fourteenth century. This was the founder of the Sikh religion—Guru Nanak. He came to destroy the superstitious beliefs and observances that were rampant amongst the people, and establish a faith based upon the perfect equality of mankind. He directed the thought and aspiration of man towards the one God who is the Lord of the universe. His is a religion that turns men into heroes of Divinity. He teaches: Devotion, love and service as the means to attain God.

> He who has fashioned the vessel of the body and poured into it
> His ambrosial gifts,
> Will only be satisfied with man's love and service.

Guru Nanak lays great emphasis upon the need of a spiritual Preceptor and holds the Divine Name, Satnam, as the mainstay of a true aspirant. That self-surrender is the goal of all spiritual strivings. That to behold the supreme will of the Almighty, as determining all events and happenings in the world, is the condition of a selfless life, filled with purity, peace and service.

Guru Nanak's mysticism, therefore reaches the very summit of spiritual experience. It is characteristic of all true mystics that they are ever fired with an invincible spirit of optimism. God is for them a most benevolent and merciful Deity, and they have discovered Him in the chamber of their own heart. They sing of Him and meditate on Him with such a fervour and ecstasy that they lose themselves in Him to realise their perfect identity with Him. Guru Nanak is indeed a veritable sun among such mystics. Here, in these few verses, we have his whole philosophy.

By Guru's teaching the light becomes manifest:

> Let us with reverence meditate
> Upon His True and Holy Name
> And also on His majesty.
>
> Who His commandments understands
> Is from all selfness free.
>
> All seasons are good for those who love the True one.
>
> He is realised
> Only through His own grace Divine.
> Who boast of other ways and means
> They idle prattlers are and false.
>
> The Precious Jewel for which man goes on pilgrimage, dwelleth within the heart.
>
> I would through His Name mount His stairs
> And reach Him, be one with Him.

Guru Nanak's powerful influence has brought into being a sect whose home is the brave province of the Punjab. He has created in the hearts of his followers the magnificent virtues of nobility, courage, toleration and equality.

May Guru Nanak's gentle and radiant spirit ever hover over mankind and pour on them the light of grace, goodwill and peace.

The Divine Life, pp. 181-182

Nature Smiles—God Smiles

The pagoda flower waves in the breeze and nods high above other tiny blossoms; the little bird, dark in colour with a black beak and yellow patch on its glossy breast, is playing and skipping, dipping now and then its wee beak into the opened petals of the tilting pagoda. The big green leaves are throbbing to the response of the mild wind.

The distant coconut branches, long and lean, are trembling in the air: the light-tinted roses and deep red flowers, the green, yellow and crimson leaves of crotons, lend charm to the scene. The mango and neem trees, tall and stately, seem to bend over each other for a friendly communion.

The platinum sky, in which are floating thin and transparent clouds, bestows a subdued brightness to the landscapes down below.

Nature smiles—God smiles.

My heart is aglow with joy when I witness this wondrous phenomena, God revelling in His own beauty and luxuriance.

On the extensive green meadows, the famished cattle graze on the lavish offering of green grass by the bounteous Mother Earth, and wax fat and strong.

O God of plenty and abundance! None can rival Thee in Thy rich, free and reckless liberality. Thou art marvellous in Thy infinite variety—in shapes, colours, movements, ways and natures.

I saw and saw and my dazed eyes become dim, and I beheld a halo spread over all space that resolved the multifaced worlds into one radiance, one presence and one truth.

Again the sun peeps out of the clouds shedding lustre on all the motley scenes of the earth, bringing out in soothing relief the varied beauty of nature against a splendrous background.

Oh, the bewitching pictures that flit before my wide open eyes, I gaze with unconcealed amazement, drinking in the enthralling panorama. Now my eyes close slowly, charmed with the soothing sweetness of the intoxication that is past expression.

O glorious World Master! O Thou Supreme Artist and Architect, O exquisite Dancer, the great Lover and Beloved! Thou who poureth Thy most heart-captivating celestial music, Thou art the enchanter who casteth Thy spell on all beings, drowning them in Thy eternal symphony; I bow to Thee who art divine wisdom, infinite love, almighty power and transcendent beauty.

Then I open my eyes, O! my Mother Divine—life and soul of the Universe, Thou showereth on us all Thy love that knows no bounds—a love that encompasses and absorbs us into Thy ecstatic Being—a love that transforms us into Thy likeness—that ultimately melts us entirely into Thy supreme Being.

The sun, moon, stars and all the heavenly bodies shine in the firmament as Thyself, revealed in a million forms. Infinite Thy bodies and Thy powers while all the time Thou art nameless and formless.

I close again my eyes and lo! that moment the universe disappears in me—lost in my immutable existence—the senses stilled and body forgotten—what peace, what joy—what rare ecstasy!

The Divine Life, pp. 43-45

Pain and Sorrow Purify Your Heart

In the play of external nature, the so-called changes, losses and failures are inevitable. If it were not so, the universal divine game would not be there before you. Therefore, view all things as a dispassionate witness and find your union and oneness with the all-inclusive Swarup of God. Play the part which God has set for you in the spirit of perfect submission to His will through all the vicissitudes of life. The object of human life is to liberate it from its self-imposed limitation and bondage, by mingling it with the eternal and ever free Reality, taking all your activities as a spontaneous and playful movement of the Divine Shakti that works within you and everywhere. To attain this freedom means to behold the same Truth revealed in all beings, creatures and things in the world, which is at once manifest and unmanifest. Sorrow and pain having been completely conquered, your life now becomes the very expression and movement of immortal bliss.

Do not forget that you live and move in a world which is really a passing show. Do not be attached to it, nor be in any way identified with it. Take the whole world-game for what it is worth. God is the only Reality, the only Truth—and to reach Him is the one principal aim of existence. When you have sincerely struggled for and have ultimately attained Him, you will have fulfilled the mission of your life. Keep up a constant and unbroken remembrance of God, and dispel from your mind the darkening influences of doubt and sorrow.

Do not go over the past. The voracious time has swallowed it up. Let the future not worry you, since what is ordained is sure to take place. In the present, take heart, having perfect trust in the Almighty. Your faith in God be the healing balm for the sharp pains of life. Faith is no faith if it cannot grant you endurance, resignation and peace.

God is ever busy in freeing you from the tangle of worldly friendship and attachments which are in their very nature unstable and unreliable, and, therefore, bring you nothing but sorrows and anxieties. Let this experience teach you that if there is one whom you can entirely trust and for whom you should offer the love of an undivided heart, it should be the supreme Lord Himself who has His eternal seat in your heart.

God is all merciful. Pray to Him. "O God, lead me from the unreal to the Real; from darkness to Light; from death to Immortality." When He makes you pass through many a painful ordeal of life, it is only to awaken you to the ultimate Reality. World is a great school of experience; but it is impermanent, it is unreal. Kunti Devi, mother of the Pandavas, prayed for pain and trouble, so that she may ever remember the Lord. Pain and sorrow purify your heart and free you from illusions. Then it is that you are eager and earnest in your quest for an existence beyond the tribulations of this world. Merciful and loving God is, when He sets you on this quest; but the path leading to it is fraught with severe trials—a necessary condition for the attainment of the divine goal. Behind all this turmoil—acute pangs of misery, anxiety and suffering—there is a spotless state of absolute peace. That is your goal. All pass away, but He who is that absolute peace is eternal.

Suffering is the very spice of life. Suffering is the glorious dawn that heralds the coming of the blazing sun and a brilliant day of absolute freedom and joy. Verily, blessed is he for whom suffering is no suffering. Surely he is now enjoying the very nectar of immortal bliss and peace.

Body is a queer instrument. It is subject to all sorts of disorders. This is true in the case of everybody. Be conscious always that you have a body and not that you are the body. This practice of dissociation from the body will set the physical machine right.

Glimpses of Divine Vision, pp. 14-19

The Pathless Path

There are various cults, creeds, sects and institutions in the world which presume to lead the struggling soul to the haven of spiritual liberation and peace. Innumerable also are the ways, methods and disciplines prescribed for purifying and elevating the spirit so that it may reach the goal of divine perfection. Aspirants are everywhere engaged in practising these methods and endeavouring to attain their object. They feel that they are caught in the grip of one or the other discipline and after some trial find that their progress is not satisfactory. Their hearts remain as impure as ever and their minds continue to be restless. If for a moment they gain some peace, again the spirit gets into a whirl and there is a feeling of frustration and despair. Some of the aspirants are tremendously earnest in their quest of immortality and peace. There are others whose aspiration is not so strong and steady. There are still others who make a show of religiosity. But all of them are dwelling in a state of uncertainty and confusion. They feel as if they are moving in the dark, groping for the real way that takes them to light and freedom. They delude themselves into the belief that they will be able to fulfil their quest in the near future.

It is true that all experiences, however bitter they may be, through which the soul passes, are necessary for its upward growth and evolution. Struggle is indeed a sure condition of progress, but the sooner the soul finds a way out of the labyrinth of confused ideas relating to the spiritual path, the better for him or her.

The true way is not a specified cut and dry method. It does not consist in joining any cult or society, in ceremonies, rituals, or bizarre phenomena. The path is simple if it can be called a path. Invite God who is all love and mercy to take you up and transform you into His radiant and blissful child. Permit His grace to purify, vitalise and take possession of every part of your being. Surrender your all to Him and be conscious of His presence within you and without you.

If you are a real spiritual aspirant, your longing for Him should be sufficiently intense to call down His grace. You should be free from the illusions of this ephemeral world. Your soul should hunger to realise its inherent divine nature. There is no purpose gained by calling yourself this or that, and by donning robes of a particular religious denomination. Masks are useless. Pretension and hypocrisy is self-deception. Break off from all clutches. Come out from the cages of your own making. Come into the open with an unfettered mind, and with the ego vanquished resign yourself to the supreme Truth residing within you. Let your vision expand and develop the universe and beyond. Let your heart embrace all beings in the folds of infinite love. Let your body work imbued with the omnipotent power of the Divine. Let every atom of your frame thrill with spiritual ecstasy and produce universal harmony. All else is unprofitable talk. All other ways lead nowhere. Do not be deceived.

Do not be a slave of wealth, name and fame. All earthly attainments and possessions pass away. Make God your aim and your goal. You are one with Him. Know this and attain real happiness and peace.

The Pathless Path, pp. viii-x

Peace is an Internal State of the Soul

Your search is for peace. Peace is an internal state of the soul acquired through the realisation of the highest Truth, which is inherent in every human being. Peace relates to the eternal. The transient and the ephemeral things of the world are incapable of granting peace. If you would have peace, turn your mind to the immortal source of your life—the deathless and changeless Reality. By constant contemplation and meditation, tune your thought to this Reality, ultimately sublimate it into that Divine existence and thereby attain to a peace which knows no change.

God is peace, Truth is peace. So be the devotee of God, if you long for peace. Live and act for the sake of this peace and having possessed it, spread its cooling radiance around, bathing all about you in its blissful floods. First, gain the God of peace for yourself. Be liberated from the clutches of a restless spirit which has thrown the soul into darkness and chaos.

Raise every thought and emotion towards the supreme seat of light, power and peace. Enter into the deepest realms of utter silence and repose of the Godhead. Associate in all manner of ways with this transcendent, all-pervading and static being of the Godhead. By entire dedication be one with Him.

Soar up with the wings of burning aspiration to the immortal throne of peace and find there the tranquillity and calmness for which you have struggled so far. Nowhere else can you attain it, for nowhere else does it exist.

O lovers of peace, everlasting peace is your birthright. The kingdom of peace is within you, nay, you are the very mould and expression of that immutable Truth. Seek not outside for this greatest consummation of life. Taste the nectar of peace in the recess of your being. There resides the heavenly light that lends splendour and beauty to all things.

Fill your heart with the pure emotions of love and compassion. Illumine your intellect with the light of eternal wisdom. Surcharge your actions with the spirit of spontaneous service and sacrifice. Then only the Divine peace that passeth all understanding will be yours unto eternity. You will then be the very embodiment of absolute peace. Your life will shine like the full moon in a cloudless sky. You will reach the sublimest acme of life's attainment!

The Divine Life, pp. 76-77

Peace is Ever Within You

The peace you crave for is ever within you. If you seek for it without, you will never have it anywhere. This is a great truth which very few realise.

Surrender is the only way to peace. So, in all circumstances of life, submit to the will of God, and be free from the touches of worry and anxiety of every kind. All happen as determined by the Lord. Do not assert your will and expect everything to take place as you wish. Unpleasant situations are the common lot of mankind. Yours is to resign yourself to the Lord and remain unaffected by them.

When the mind rests in peace by a complete self-surrender, the heart's desire is realised without any delay. The longing ceases by a perfect self-abandonment, and then no time is lost for its fruition. This is the secret of realisation.

The one predominant hunger of the soul is for absolute peace and bliss. You can have this peace and bliss only when your mind rests on the bosom of the Infinite Reality. So, a constant contemplation or thought of the great Truth whose attributes are immortal bliss and peace can alone completely satisfy the yearning of the soul. Direct, therefore, all the forces of your mind and intellect towards the All-merciful Lord of the universe, and put yourself entirely into His hands. There is no path easier than self-surrender. He who trusts the Almighty never comes to any harm. This is the rule of God that knows no exception. Do therefore walk the path of pure and simple devotion. Be conscious that the Lord seated in your heart is your all-powerful protector. Keep Him ever in your remembrance. Tune your thought and life with His radiant existence, and thus permit His divine energy to flow into you and transform your life into one of peace and joy. Don't give yourself away to dejection, doubt and despair.

To experience the stillness of the all-pervading Spirit who is at once the witness of this world of manifestation and the world-manifestation itself is to realise God in His all-inclusive nature and being. Behold Divinity everywhere. Rise above all conditions and dwell ever in union with the immortal Truth who has become all. Everything is His doing because all, all is He alone. Ramdas has nothing beyond this to tell you. Realise that you and all beings, creatures and things in the world are utterly divine.

It is absolutely of no avail for a man to bewail over his worldly lot and his unstable attachments to worldly friends. Seek the true life in God, and the friendship of the Eternal—the highest; both are everlasting. The real peace can never come to the share of man so long as he thinks that the adjustments of external life can grant him happiness. Disappointment and misery must be his lot wherever he be. Take thought and know once for all that real freedom and peace lie only in the close communion with the immortal Truth dwelling in your heart. Take complete refuge in God through constant remembrance of Him, and thus be content in all situations He places you. Don't embitter your life with thoughts of worry and care. Make God your friend and aid. Once you become His, He never gives you up. He takes you to the seat of immortality and bliss. This is the way and there is no other.

True it is that until a man or a woman has found in his or her heart the beloved Lord of the universe, there can be no real peace and liberation for the struggling soul. Therefore, feel always that the divine Presence is ever with you and in you. Let the stream of His remembrance flow continuously in your mind, and may you attain the supreme blessedness of perfect union with Him.

Glimpses of Divine Vision, pp. 44-49

Pray to Him, Sing of Him

Call on the Lord with all the love of your heart. Concentrate all your longing in that call, and you may be sure that God will respond. Thus it was His great devotees of the past and present entitled themselves to His infinite grace. The language of love is simply irresistible. Just as the child by its lisping talks, charms and captures the heart of the mother, so the true devotee by his frank and plaintive words of love draws towards him the Almighty Beloved of his heart. The language of the devotee is the expression of his pure and aspiring heart. Heart is the Vina and devotion the fingers that play upon it to infuse a magic spell in the call for the Beloved. Hence the devotee employs sweet music for his appeals and prayers to God. He cries and weeps for God, extols and glorifies Him, talks and holds communion with Him—in a rhythmic language of love. He sings and dances when he has found his Beloved. The music of Divine symphony thrills his entire frame. Ecstasy or inexpressible joy rises in waves in his heart. Love overflows in tears through his eyes. Purity, peace and light permeate his entire being. This is the culmination of his utter devotion and self-surrender. He places his entire life, soul and body at the feet of the Beloved. How does the devotee attain to this exalted state of perfect union with the Lord of his heart? It is clear that he adopts music as the means by which he tunes his heart with the heart of Lord. A heart that is filled with love—selfless and radiant—alone raises a human being to the feet of the Almighty. Such a love sings like the nightingale, gives out perfume like the rose, beautifies life in all its aspects, and brings the devotee in intimate touch and eternal fellowship with the Lord.

Therefore, call on the Lord with all your heart and He is sure to respond. Make Him the sole beloved of your life and He is sure to be yours. Pray to Him, sing of Him, dedicate yourself to Him, and He will grant you absolute peace and bliss—nay, He will reveal Himself in your heart and absorb you into His transcendent being, and thus make you realise that you are the very embodiment of His own cosmic peace and joy. He will then give you the vision of beholding Him everywhere, i.e. you will behold your own supreme Self manifested as the entire universe. Love is your way and love is your goal.

Call on the Lord—the Beloved. Have you found anything sweeter than His Name, more charming than the sound of His Name? If you have real love for the Lord you will reply: "Certainly, I have not." Then there is no need for anybody to tell you that you should sing on His Name and be inebriated with the Divine ecstasy associated with it. You will find your life has changed into a song of eternity. Who could adequately describe in words the wonderful glory of the Beloved's Name? He who has tasted alone knows what it is like. Oh! taste it and let the Name illuminate your heart and intellect and fill you with floods of joy. Sing on His Name with all love and devotion and embrace the Beloved in the recesses of your heart. What blessedness then is yours! Can you now hold such a precious possession in comparison with all the riches of the world? Name, fame and wealth in this evanescent world are as nothing to you when your heart has once drunk the nectar of the Beloved's Name. Therefore, sing on His Name with one-pointed devotion. The Beloved awaits you: you have only to take His Name and He runs to you. How simple it is, yet how difficult with many whose love for the Beloved is not as intense as their attachment to the perishable baubles of the world!

Direct your thought within and listen to the call of your own voice and the responsive word of the Beloved will come to you, and you will discover that He is within you. Verily, the Beloved is in the heart of His devotee. Mingle your life in the ocean of His existence. Expand your heart to meet the infinity of His love. Widen your vision so that you may be bathed in His light, power and joy. Now you have become the Beloved's beloved. Now you are one with Him. Oh! the power and greatness of the call! Call on Him, sing of Him and be ever blessed!

The Divine Life, pp. 129-131

Prayer: What is the Best Prayer?

Devotee: *When we pray to God, what should we ask for?*

Ramdas: Ask for nothing of the world. If at all you pray for anything, address God thus: 'Oh God, in my foolishness I may be asking for many things. Be gracious enough not to grant my prayers. Give me only whatever you think is best for me.' This is the best prayer.

Gospel of Swami Ramdas, p. 500

Pride is the Greatest Weakness

The greatest weakness of a human being lies in his presumption and pride. By this frailty he falls prey to every conceivable hardship, mortification and sorrow. Therefore, men of wisdom have extolled the virtue of humility. The pliant grass on the meadow, when even the most violent breezes blow over it, does not come to grief; it bends before the blast, and touching the ground raises its head again, perfectly free from any harm. Whilst the stiff and unyielding tree, subjected to a stormy wind, breaks down and is thrown on the ground; its puny resistance against the mighty power of the wind brings about its woeful plight. Similarly, the man who is puffed up with conceit like the tree, courts through ignorance, pain and misery.

Man speaks of love and goodwill in glowing terms. He holds out meekness as an essential means to the attainment of peace. But where his own peace is concerned or that of others, he flouts at his own preaching and lives contrary to the highest principles of life which his voice of intuition has set for him. Pride swallows up all the beautiful things of his nature. An uncompromising hardness and a darkening inertness seize his heart and intellect. Now comes the downfall.

Before the Almighty will, before the wisdom of the Infinite, before the sublimity of the supreme Reality, man who poses himself to be clever, good and wise is worse than dust. A blade of grass, by its silent example, teaches such a one what a true life is and should be.

Man's quest is for peace. Peace can dwell in that heart alone which is totally bereft of the poisoning influence of pride. The way of liberation from the clutches of the evil pride, is to turn the mind within, so that it can know what its real worth is. A steady gaze at the eternal truth of his being within will exorcise the demon that has possessed him.

Saints and great teachers of Truth are, and have been, condemning in emphatic and unmistakable words this monster who has wrecked and ruined many a soul in the world.

What is the direct method by which pride overthrows even the wisest men? The first thing pride does is to generate in the mind passions of the wildest kind. Life is now thrown into a whirl of confused activity bringing on the soul drunk with pride a state bordering on lunacy.

If universal love is your creed, O man, strive first to obtain the peace of the eternal. If you would have this peace, put on the purifying garment of humility. Blessed are the poor in spirit, because theirs and theirs only is the Truth.

The Divine Life, pp. 103-104

Ramana Maharshi was a Saviour of Souls

A sun of rare spiritual brilliance has set. Sri Ramana Maharshi renounced His body on the night of the 14th April, 1950 at His Ashram in Tiruvannamalai. His passing away has produced a most conspicuous void in our world today. Thousands of His devotees in India and foreign countries are feeling the loss most sorrowfully. We can take consolation in the fact that since Sri Ramana, as the Supreme Spirit, is imperishable, He dwells always in the hearts of us all. For, He was the very incarnation of the Divine.

Sri Ramana was a Saviour of souls. The men and women who went to Him for spiritual illumination, returned with their hearts filled with divine peace and joy. His look was most dynamic. When He cast His gaze on any aspirant, who stood, or sat before Him, it electrified the person and entirely turned the course of his life Godwards. Sometimes it shook the very foundation of that person's life and surcharged it with unutterable peace and ecstasy. Vast numbers, from different countries and nationalities, today look up to Him as a great redeeming spiritual force that would bring about a regeneration in the life of humanity.

Sri Ramana's philosophy is very simple. He asks you to find out "WHO AM I?" This self-enquiry directly turns your mind inward and makes you realise the truth that the individual 'I' to which you are so perversely clinging has no existence. In other words, the self-enquiry enables you to completely dissolve the ego-sense and grants you at once the consciousness of the Reality. You now know that you are the supreme Atman—the one, eternal, indivisible, all-pervading and blissful Truth.

Here Ramdas must say a few words about his personal contact with Sri Ramana. It was 27 years ago (in 1923) that Ramdas was drawn to Him and had the brief contact of about five minutes with Him. But these five minutes were for him pregnant with immense spiritual significance and possibility. When Sri Ramana intently gazed on Ramdas and the eyes of both met, Ramdas felt He was pouring into him His spiritual power and grace in abundance, so much so that Ramdas was thrilled, as His divine light shone on his mind, heart and soul. Sri Ramana's eyes always radiated a splendour, which was simply unique and irresistible—a splendour mingled with infinite tenderness, compassion and mercy. The few minutes that Ramdas spent in His holy company meant a momentous impetus in his spiritual career.

With the above few words of loving tribute to Sri Ramana Maharshi, Ramdas offers his humble salutations to Him. May His Spirit ever illumine the hearts of all His devotees is the earnest prayer of His child.

The Divine Life, pp. 192-193

Reality Which is Deathless and Changeless

In this evanescent panorama of life all things and objects are subject to transmutation and dissolution. The Lord alone is real with whom we are eternally united.

Do not seek to find peace and freedom in external circumstances of life, because true freedom is of the mind only, when you are in tune with God, who dwells within you. Let the knocks and hits of life turn you more and more towards God, so that you can become impervious to all kinds of outside attacks upon you. Take the name of the Lord with all strength and faith. Repeat it breathlessly, as it were, at all times, whether you are at your bath, in the kitchen, on the road or in the office. In this, lies the way of your escape. Know this fact once for all and take refuge in the Name.

God is a living Reality. He is more real than the ephemeral interests and things in which man is usually involved. Man's cravings for the earthly achievements shuts him out from the recognition of immortal Truth of his existence. He is so deeply caught in pleasures which are gained through mere sense perception and touch that he becomes blind to the exalted experience of eternal Bliss and Peace....

So, O beloved soul, unless you link your life with the divine Author of your being, your life is in vain.

Life is a short span and the pleasures you derive in it are transient and fleeting. In pursuing these shadows you are heading towards darkness and are becoming oblivious to the exalted and ever-blissful Truth which is your real being.

Man is miserable because he seeks joy and peace in external conditions and objects which are in their very nature incapable of yielding the perfect state for which the heart of man longs.

Your happiness or misery depends on your state of mind and not upon your external conditions or circumstances. When your mind impelled by desires is flitting from object to object, craving for possession and enjoyment, it lives in a state of restlessness which itself is misery. After possession of the object, come cares and anxieties, after its loss follow grief and pain. The small amount of happiness you derive here is like a tiny, flickering light in a thick, vast mass of darkness; it dies out in a moment only to envelop you in a worse enthralling gloom. Know this; the object you crave for is perishable and transient in itself. How then can lasting peace be derived from it? Hence when the mind wanders in the midst of this ever-changing, impermanent medley of forms and things, it experiences nothing but pain and sorrow. Now then, direct your vision inward and behold God within—that eternal seat of all bliss and peace.

Peace is in that heart in which no wave of desire of any kind rises, and it is to be understood, that the true aspiration of the heart is completely to quell and still down all desires that lurk in it and which cause dissatisfaction, turmoil and misery. Peace, peace, peace is the cry of the heart—a peace which wants nothing, a peace that is self-existent —a peace that is immortal. This eternal peace is your real existence—it is not a state or truth to be attained but to be realised; because you are ever That.

The transient and ephemeral things of the world are incapable of granting peace. If you would have peace, turn your mind to the immortal source of your life—the deathless and changeless Reality. By constant contemplation and meditation, tune your thought to the Reality, ultimately sublimate it into that divine existence and thereby attain to a peace which knows no change.

We may live for thousands of years and may obtain whatever we desire of the world, but we shall never be happy so long as our hunger for earthly things does not perish.

Renounce all desires of the mind and intellect and enjoy the bliss of the Atman even though you may, for its sake, live in a garret, or even turn into a wandering and naked mendicant.

The Pathless Path, pp. 3-5

Reborn in a New and Glorious Life

Truth or God demands of us the highest sacrifice. It is a bid for immortality or everlasting life. Such a life can never be ours unless we dedicate ourselves entirely for the realisation of it. We have before us the instances of innumerable sages and saints of the world who have attained to this immortal life by nothing short of a complete and all-round self-consecration. A close study of their lives reveals to us the one predominant fact that they have surrendered up their heart, soul and body to the supreme Power that lies at the basis of all creation. The personal clingings, the false attachments, narrow ideals and individual desires have all been given up for a life of infinite vision, imbued with a consciousness of perfect freedom and peace. So it is that the devotee of God can be His only when the devotee looks upon Him as his all in all. He thereafter lives and moves in a region pre-eminently exalted, transcending the superficial crust of life. His life thus becomes a continuous round of indescribable felicity and Divine rapture.

The result of this great conversion is an inevitable feeling in the heart of the transformed being that he is reborn in a new and glorious life. His dwelling in the infinite grants him an elevation, a lightness, a freedom which are distinctly the qualities of an eternal existence. In truth he now lives a very God upon this earth.

Let us remember once more that God demands of us a supreme sacrifice. The notion of 'I' and 'mine' must be obliterated from the mind to its last touch or vestige. The struggling spirit must find complete contentment, peace and repose in the eternal and tranquil bosom of the Divine Master and Mother of the worlds. What prevents one from such an integral dedication is the attraction to the ephemeral objects of life—the ties that bind one to the mortal or passing phases of life.

A soul fired with a burning zeal and an unconquerable heroism can alone cross the boundary and enter the kingdom of eternal joy and peace. Just as an unshapen stone can be fashioned into a beautiful image worthy of adoration and worship only after it has received many a stroke of the chisel, so also a distorted and inharmonious life has to pass through many a trial, suffering and tribulation before the great change could come over it, before the life of ignorance could be transmuted into a life of immortal splendour and joy, fit to be revered and adored.

We speak of Divine Love. The possession of this Love can never be for one who has retained his individual predispositions, who is harbouring the ideals of a selfish outlook, who is wedded to the things that perish, who is caught in the toils of a confused understanding and a heart unleavened with compassion and peace. So purification of the heart and mind by charging it with the spirit of Love for all creatures and beings in the world is the first step that brings about the Divine transformation. The light of Truth can shine in the soul and flood the entire being only when knowledge dawns in the mind and love fills the heart. Dedication is thus the substitution of a lower for a higher life, of death for immortality, of bondage for liberation, of sorrow for ever-abiding peace and bliss. The soul is for ever free from the bonds of the body and mind.

The Divine Life, pp. 128-129

Religion is a Matter of Experience

The path to the source of your and the world's being is not without. You have to go within yourself. You must go past your senses, mind and intellect; you must traverse beyond all your ideas and ideals; you must transcend all limits, conditions and tastes, and then alone will you have the fullest vision and realisation of your immortal root. This immortal root is also the root of all that exists—the visible and the invisible worlds and all beings and creatures in them.

Religion is a matter of experience. Merely by becoming a member of a church, creed or sect, a person cannot be entitled to this experience. By reading any amount of scriptures and sacred books he cannot obtain this experience. By the observance of rites, ceremonies, or worship a man cannot come by this experience. Spiritual realisation is a question of individual effort and struggle...... The man of true religion when he is on the path, is mainly concerned with his own internal struggle for liberation and peace.

A steady, persevering and concentrated effort and struggle alone can lead the aspirant to the realisation of God. So long as a man is hankering after the pleasures of the senses, his progress on the path is slow and erratic. He must be undaunted in his endeavour and determined in his purpose. He must leave no stone unturned to subdue and eventually eradicate the impure passions of his heart and mind. A purified and enlightened Buddhi alone can entitle the Sadhaka to enter the kingdom of eternity.

What is required principally is the withdrawal of the mind from without to within, which means that the restless and roaming nature of the mind must be totally curbed by right thought, right contemplation and right meditation. The mind has to settle down and its uncontrolled dynamics must be brought under subjection. Perseverance and an unflagging endeavour are the qualities of a true aspirant or seeker of Truth. Lassitude, idleness and heedlessness are the enemies of spiritual progress. Awareness, watchfulness and effort are the true qualities of a Sadhaka.

The Pathless Path, pp. 8-9

Religion is an Intensely Practical Thing

All creatures including human beings are by nature active and prolific, and the ordinary life of everyone in the world is a whirlpool of continuous movement in its physical and manifest nature. The rush of activity has so far absorbed the lives of all people on this planet, and to such an extent that eternal values that stand at the basis of human and all existence are in the majority of cases entirely ignored. Thus you find so much strife and chaos in the world as observed at the present time. Although every endeavour is made to harmonize life and so adjust its activities as to produce peace and happiness, we find the results achieved are far from the desired end. The reason is quite clear. So long as the aspiring heart of man is caught in the toils of mere confused activity of his lower nature, so long as his vision is only for the apparent and evanescent pleasures and ambitions of life, without a deep understanding of the fundamental principle on which his life is built, he cannot hope to infuse into his activities the true spirit of the higher and abiding light and joy of the immortal.

A true life, if it should be blessed with this splendour of its immortality, must be inspired with a consciousness of its deathless and changeless nature. So to control and guide life by an internal attuning of it with the universal spirit of God is the only right way to live life. Be in touch with the supreme truth of your being and, understanding the exalted purpose and goal of life, work out your destiny on the lines of love, kindness and charity. Religion is not of mere books or talk or a thing for reflection. Religion is an intensely practical thing—a revealment of the inherent supremacy of the soul in all the turns of human life. You may belong to any sect, creed or faith, you may call yourself by any name or denomination, you may belong to any religious society but if you do not put into practice the highest ideals set forth by your great Teachers and live up to their magnificent examples in actual life and action, your profession of religion is of no avail. Your life is a current that is started from an eternal source. Make it flow in all its pristine purity so that it may lighten the burden of the weak, relieve the distress of the suffering, elevate the hearts of the depressed and in short bring sunshine and delight in the prevailing darkness of the world. With a firm will destroy all the inimical tendencies that seek to thwart this sweet and glorious consummation, conquer every selfish craving that tries to pull you down from your upward march towards the summit of this blessedness, eradicate from the heart all disruptive forces that conspire to keep you in your lower animal nature and, ultimately rising superior to them all, realise the sublimity of your Divine Self and thus illumine your life with the light, love and bliss of God.

The Divine Life, pp. 14-15

Religion is as Vast as the Very Heavens

Religion, whose function is to guide and inspire mankind towards a life of mutual understanding, help and friendliness, has strangely been the cause of racial hatreds, destructive rivalries and false attitudes of superiority.

We want a religion shorn off all its narrow particularisations, and free from dogmatic beliefs, superstitious impositions and bigoted and sanctimonious ways. We want a religion which appeals to the inner spirit of every man and woman—a religion which is universal in its outlook and embraces all alike within its fold. We want a religion which brings love and joy to our heart, and light and wisdom to our head. We want a religion that knits man to man, irrespective of any apparent distinctions, into a common human community on the earth. We want a religion that teaches us to sacrifice our little joys for the service of the distressed humanity. We want a religion that would give us the sight to behold all the members of the human race as belonging to one world family. We want a religion that makes us realise that we are the immortal, all-pervading and ever-blissful Spirit, and that God, we and universe are one in the absolute Reality. We want a religion that would make us offer our homage equally to all the Teachers and Incarnations of the different creeds and sects in the world.

Religion is, in its real sense, as vast as the very heavens which grants refuge to all alike; as accessible to all as the very air that fills all space; and as equal in granting its favours to everyone as the light of the sun. You cannot confine religion within the narrow walls of a creed or society. So to be the votary of true religion means to be utterly free from all cramping limitations and to come out in the open to grip the hand of a Hindu, a Christian, a Moslem, a Parsi, a Buddhist, a Jain and a Jew with the same equal love and vision.

The keynote of a religious life is selfless service—a service born of pure love and compassion for all beings and creatures on this earth. It is only such Divinely inspired men and women who can stand forth as the champions of peace and goodwill, because they are possessed with the exalted vision of life eternal. Every human being can raise himself to this spiritual splendour and peace. He has only to break through the shell of egotism and reveal himself as he is—snap the bonds of the flesh and enter into his immortal life of the Spirit. Thus liberated he speaks out:

> "Peace and joy being your inherent possession, why go out of yourself in pursuit of them? Being the light yourself, why do you grope in darkness longing for an outer changing ray, why deny your own everlasting radiance? Know that you are the Soul of the very universe—the eternal light, peace and joy. Realise your light and illuminate all. Realise your peace and shower tranquillity on all. Say 'I am the all-blissful Spirit' and shed your joy on all. Assert your Divine nature and liberate thousands and millions from the fetters of bondage. Be God and lead others to God.
>
> Love all and hate none. Mere talk of peace will avail you nothing. Mere talk of God and religion will not take you far. Bring out all the latent powers of your being and reveal the full magnificence of your immortal Self. Be surcharged with peace and joy and scatter them wherever you are and wherever you go. Be a blazing

flame of Truth, be a beauteous blossom of love and be a soothing balm of peace. By the power of your Spirit dispel the darkness of ignorance, dissolve the clouds of discord and war and bring goodwill, peace and harmony amongst the people of the globe. This is your mission in life.

Live not for passing phantasies of life. Bid for immortality by dedicating all the forces of it to the service of God in humanity. Away with petty ambitions. Away with a low and narrow vision of life. Arise in all the glory and majesty of your invincible Self. Be pure, selfless, patient and resigned, never allow the ego to raise its hood and drag you after it; but be full of power, grace and splendour of God, verily you are God."

This is what true religion should make of a human being, all else is vanity and vexation.

The Divine Life, pp. 6-8

Renunciation is an Inner State of Mind

Sannyas, as Ramdas understands it, is a means to an end. It signifies a complete detachment from the objects of senses and a total indifference to worldly activities. The mind must be free from the hankering for sense pleasures and the body liberated from actions done with a view to gain any fruit or reward. This constitutes renunciation which is essential for fixing our mind on God and God alone.

The life thereafter is lived only for realising Him—to attain the supreme state of perfect peace and joy. Uninterrupted or unbroken communion and contemplation of God alone can enable the soul to know its identity with the Divine. It is only then that the heart of the seeker will be filled with divine love, compassion and peace.

Life has not only to be illumined in its inner consciousness, but is must also be imbued with divine splendour in all its external expressions and movements. So all disciplines, prayers, meditation and dedication, are gone through with the sole object of transcending the physical and the mental, the animal and the human planes, into the divine plane by the experience of which the soul obtains an all-round spiritual achievement. In this illumined state there is neither renunciation of the world, nor the enjoyment of it. The Sannyasin aims at attaining this highest all-comprehensive wisdom and salvation.

The beauty and magnificence of this supreme realisation of God are evident in the life of one who is thoroughly egoless, always absorbed in a supernal light, love and joy, and remains so in all situations and conditions. He is in the world, but not of the world. He acts and at the same time acts not. He identifies himself with all beings and creatures and so his love flows out towards all alike. His eyes are radiant with the vision of Truth and he beholds himself manifest as all objects in the universe.

Such a one has no particular mark, garb, or denomination to single him out. He is free from all bondages, conventions and rules of any order, sect creed or religion. He is a universalist. Once this goal is reached, all the chains that bound him either to the worldly life, or to the life, later adopted, of self-discipline, automatically fall away from him. His purity is now not a relative acquisition, which is maintained by the observance of any rule, vow or control; but it is a natural state born of the realisation of his pristine spiritual beauty, sanctity and peace.

So Sannyas, or any other method of approach to God, employed by various seekers of Truth, is only a means by adopting which the soul seeks liberation from the thraldom of lust, greed and wrath, and experiences the fullness and glory of its integral spiritual life and being. It is not by mere external renunciation that one attains God. There are so many who have externally renounced and gone to the forests, but have not realised Him. It is not necessary that one should externally renounce anything. It is not the outer condition that matters so much as one's inner state of mind. If we dedicate our life to God and live in His light, it does not matter where we live. We can live in the family and still realise Him, because God is everywhere and not only in the forests and caves. He is in us, with us and all about us. To seek Him, we need not go anywhere.

The examples of Buddha, Chaitanya and Vivekananda are not for all to follow. They are rare cases in which God made them renounce the external ties also, so that they might freely serve all mankind. When God wants us to undertake such a glorious mission, by all means, let us not resist the current when it comes to sweep away our narrow limitations. Sri Krishna and

Janaka, in their lives, have shown that even for the work of Lokasangraha, the normal duties of life that fall to our lot need not be abandoned. To attain Moksha for oneself, wilful breaking off from external ties is not at all necessary.

God-realisation is not getting away from the world, but looking upon it as the manifestation of God and serving Him in all creatures and beings, in a state of perfect submission to His will.

Ramdas still belongs to the world, not in a partial sense, but in totality. His Beloved is not only in particular persons, but is in His full power and glory in all beings, creatures and things. Ramdas has only expanded the narrow family circle into a world-family. So it is not renunciation, but expansion. God has in His mercy made him embrace the whole universe as his. Ramdas' Beloved dwells everywhere, as all beings and creatures in the world.

What we have to give up is the ego-sense, the idea that we are the doers. God within us is the Doer, the sole Master of all our activities. If we dedicate all our actions to Him, we can destroy our ego-sense and find our supreme union with Him. Surrender does not denote any change in the external mode of life, but a right attitude towards it.

When your heart is full of God, naturally there is no other thought in it. That is renunciation—to have no desire for anything in the world. Just as a great pond, beside a river, can be filled by opening a channel between the two, so also when you unite your mind with God, His power, love and grace will pour into you, and your mind will be full of joy, free from all desires. That joy fills you through and through from within.

The river of God with which you have to connect yourself is not without. It is within you. You have only to open the channel and you are flooded with joy. We desire material things, only because we have no contentment. We know by experience that we will not be happy by getting external things. They are followed by pain and worry. But the joy you get by communing with God is perennial. There is no break in it. It is based upon the immortal Truth within you and not on the perishable objects outside you. Perishable objects cannot give you imperishable joy. The imperishable alone can give you eternal joy and that imperishable being is God.

Question: *Have the clothes we wear any influence on the spiritual life?*

Ramdas: No, unless it be for one who has renounced desires or attachment for the world, and lives a life completely cut off from the world. For him it is important. For a seeker of Truth, not engaged in any other activities, the peculiar Gerua dress he puts on helps him to remember that his life is dedicated to God. When his dedication has become complete and realisation of God is achieved, it is immaterial what dress he puts on.

Ramdas tells this from his own experience. He was wearing ochre-coloured clothes during his early years of spiritual Sadhana or God-seeking. He continued dressing that way for about three or four years after which he gave them up, and he started wearing the white clothes commonly used by all. When he had the coloured on, he was feeling that his life was a dedicated one. The ochre colour signifies renunciation. So, whenever he looked at the cloth, he felt this life was God's and not to be used for anything else except for the realisation and service of God. Thus it was helpful, though it is not always essential.

A person can dedicate himself to God without any external changes, because the dedication is purely an internal matter. He may use any cloth he likes. It is immaterial in which way he dresses. Many saints dress themselves in the ordinary way and yet have their whole life dedicated to God. Their life is one of perfect inner renunciation.

The Divine Life, pp. 319-322

Researches into the Realm of the Soul

Man's supreme quest lies in his researches into the realm of the soul, spirit and God. The deeper he dives into the abyss of Truth the more wonderful grows his experience. He finds worlds are involved in worlds and, as he progresses inward, subtler are the planes of existence which he meets. As he passes through them he beholds supernatural visions of Divine forms; hears the sweetest strains of celestial music; senses the intoxicating fragrance of heavenly aroma; is dazzled by the flashes of immortal radiance; experiences an unutterable rapture of pure bliss, and at last reaching the utmost confines of the soul and the inner worlds plunges into the infinite expanse of a static silence and immutable peace wherein everything is nought, wherefrom everything emanates. Further journey ceases here because now the traveller and the destination have resolved into one as the river merges into the ocean. This transcendent experience makes the soul realise not merely an inner unity of all life and existence but also the absolute oneness of all visible and invisible worlds of manifestation.

Now he feels both his physical and psychical being, in all its aspects, is utterly Divine as also the vast phenomena of nature before him. The ecstasy and light of the Divine fill every pore of his body, and every atom of his physical frame responds to the thrills of delight originating from his immortal Spirit which is now one with the cosmic soul, the great basic ultimate Godhead who is all-inclusive and all-transcendent.

Love now blossoms in his heart like a full-blown flower. The world is the playground of his liberated spirit. His bliss and freedom passeth all description. Childlike innocence pervades his entire being. Divine splendour illumines his face. He rolls in ineffable ecstasy. He knows he is immortal.

The Divine Life, p. II

Saints are Verily the Redeemers of Fallen Souls

In order to attain to the supreme blessedness of life, namely the realisation of God, we have to surcharge our thought with the idea of God. God must take possession of our mind until our mind is no longer there as such and God alone is. Until this is done the aspirant must employ every means possible to control the mind and its activities so that the thought of God alone should rule in it. This thought must sink deep into the mind, transforming its fickle, restless and impure nature into the very Spirit of joy, purity and peace.

The world is hungering for this great ideal of happiness and peace. Ramdas' experience, when he was flitting from village to village, from town to town in the blessed land of Saints—Maharashtra—was, he observed not only the intensity or keenness of spiritual hunger amongst thousands of people there who came to see him but he also discovered that many of them, whatever the external circumstances, were drinking deep at the fountain of eternal joy. The chief condition needed for realising this state is unceasing hunger or uninterrupted and unbroken aspiration for the immortal.

The easiest means to make the mind dwell in the idea of God is to constantly reiterate mentally or vocally the Name of God. Such a recitation of the Name should of course be accompanied by implicit faith in the efficacy of the Name and intense love for the immortal ideal which the Name represents, viz. the supreme Reality who is absolute existence, consciousness and bliss and who is seated in the hearts of us all. When thus the mind is completely absorbed in the Divine idea, a stage is reached when the mere individual or physical consciousness is transmuted into the universal and ever blissful consciousness.

This is all right. Everybody wishes to possess this hunger, this keen aspiration which will bring him or her the experience of Divinity. But the complaint is that such a state does not come even when one wishes for it. How then could this burning desire for the attainment of absolute bliss be generated? Just as an uneducated man or a poor man would evince an ardent wish to be a literate man or a rich man when he comes in association with a learned person or a wealthy person; so also when an ignorant, bound and sorrow-stricken soul comes in contact with an illumined, liberated and all-blissful person, the former by such contact is fired with a zeal to become also like the latter. Hence the society of saints has been held as the most important factor in the spiritual evolution of the soul. The saints not only awaken the ignorant souls and create in them a thirst for self-realisation but also infuse into them by their blessings the needed spiritual strength to battle against the forces that confront the aspirant in his march towards this goal of supreme beatitude.

In order to know what are our actual facial features we have to look into the mirror; similarly, if we wish to get a glimpse of our real and immortal life we can do so only when we are in the company of saints. Saints are verily the redeemers of fallen souls. It is by their power alone the mind that runs in pursuit of transient pleasures can be made to concentrate its attention upon the eternal, changeless and blissful indwelling Reality. When thus the mind is permeated through and through with the imperishable idea of God, man attains the supreme goal of life.

God-realisation does bring about not only the divinisation of the internal life of man but also of all his external life and activities. He beholds all beings and things as the illumined expressions of the one all-pervading Divinity. Satsang awakens the human soul and fills his thought with Divine light and joy and grants him the knowledge of the immortal Self, which in its turn confers upon the devotee the comprehensive knowledge of God in all His aspects.

The Divine Life, pp. 124-125

Saints: Who is a Saint?

Who is a saint? A saint is he who has attained the Eternal, lives in the Eternal and has realised the Eternal—call the great Reality by any name—the Eternal, God or Truth. Such a saint is a veritable blessing upon this earth. By his contact thousands are saved from the clutches of doubt, sorrow and death. He lives what he preaches and preaches what he lives. He exerts a wonderful influence and creates in the hearts of ignorant men a consciousness of their inherent Divinity. He awakens the sleeping soul to the awareness of their immortal and all-blissful nature. By his very presence he rids the hearts of people of their base and unbridled passions. The faithful derive the greatest benefit by communion with him.

A veil of unreality has shrouded the human soul and so he feels that he is a weak, helpless and miserable creature. His life is therefore purposeless and vain—productive of no good to himself or to the world. Such a life can recover its Divine heritage by the touch and society of a saint. A saint is a real redeemer and saviour of a fallen soul, for a saint is God Himself manifest in flesh and blood.

It is rightly said that the one condition to be fulfilled for the redemption of a soul is the necessary faith and aspiration in the devotee on the one hand, and the requisite spiritual power in the saint to redeem the disciple on the other. A heart filled with universal compassion can alone throw out its light to enliven hope and joy where there is none. Divine compassion and love of which the heart of a saint is made are simply irresistible in their effects. Depend upon it, whenever he casts his glance on anybody or anything, he pours on them always the very nectar of love and kindness. His heart ever longs to lead the entrapped souls from the prison of darkness and ignorance into a life of joy, freedom and immortality.

The greatness of a saint is simply indescribable. We can only bend and bow to him and thus earn his ever-fruitful grace and benediction.

The Divine Life, pp. 117-118

Self-Control

A human being is made up of two natures—one Divine and the other animal. When the animal nature is predominant and rules over all his mental and physical activities, his Divine nature becomes inexpressive and latent. True happiness and freedom for man depend upon the development and ultimate revealment of his innate, higher and spiritual nature. Without understanding this, man, led blindly by his lower and self-degrading desires, falls a prey to every kind of misery, pain and bondage. Instead of conserving and concentrating the forces that work in him for self-elevation and the uplift of the world at large, he allows himself to be dominated over by the baser impulses and passions of his lower nature and reaps, as a consequence, a harvest of misfortunes, sorrows and anxieties. Such a man has really abused and wasted away a precious life granted to him.

Man's success in life can be measured only by his living a life of sacrifice and service which requires a thorough control of the mind which, when undisciplined, drags him down into the darkness of ignorance and ruin. Whereas a man who keeps his mind and senses under perfect control, and permits the inherent and latent Divine forces to express themselves in him, will be a great power that diffuses light and joy to all people who come into contact with him. If the creative principle in human nature should triumph unimpeded for producing 'the greatest good to the greatest number', a man should free himself from the clutches of selfishness and by a proper subdual of his egoistic tendencies rise to the height of his immortal existence.

Unwittingly or without understanding, he fritters away his energies in various vain pursuits. The great souls who have shed on mankind the lustre of their beneficence are men and women who have, by a continuous and unbaffled course of endeavour and discipline, gained a complete mastery over themselves. Such are the true creators in the world.

Man is not intended to live in subservience to the animal instincts in him. Principally, there are four qualities which man has in common with the animals, viz. sense of fear, sleep, sexual impulse and craving for food. If man becomes a slave to these animal tendencies and does not control them, he would be a man only in name. Whilst man has plenty of will-power to do a great deal of harm to himself and others, he pleads he is weak when he is asked to use his powerful will for directing him upwards towards the achievement of his higher, exalted and divine nature. In short, life is intended for self-control and the realisation of the Godly being that he is.

The Divine Life, pp. 106-108

Self-Realisation: Its Impact on Society

A Student: *How does Self-realisation of an individual help society?*

Ramdas: By Self-realisation you become happy inwardly and therefore seek nothing from outside. So, your activities flow out only for the uplift and good of others. A man who is discontented within seeks for external things in order to get happiness, and so doing, harms society. He thinks he will get happiness from external objects. When you have found true happiness by realising the Self, that is, by realising that your true nature is absolute peace and bliss, you are not in conflict with anybody, your vision is equal and your activities turn to the service of everyone. Then it is that you become the true instrument of God. Our little self stands in the way of our doing good to the world. Not only do we not do good, but we harm the world, as the spirit of exploitation seizes us and we do things only as prompted by the ego. After Self-realisation, our life will be entirely dedicated to the service of humanity. The happiest man is the most generous man. The miserly and selfish man, besides being miserable himself, makes others near him also unhappy.

Student: *When he gets the supreme Bliss, he indulges in it for himself. How are others benefited thereby?*

Ramdas: That is not like the enjoyment of the senses. A burning lamp cannot hide its light. So, when bliss is experienced within yourself, you spread it everywhere around you. It is not for any one individual, but for the whole universe.

A Devotee: *It is said that Self-realised beings do not move in society. Is that correct?*

Ramdas: Are you sure? If so, give an example. The great teachers were not selfish. They did not keep to themselves the spiritual knowledge they had gained. They lived in the world to elevate those who came in contact with them. Take the case of Buddha and Sankara. How much did they wander about for the uplift of the people! They did not keep away from society or remain in solitude.

Gospel of Swami Ramdas, pp. 460-461

Self-Realised Persons: Jivan Muktas

Jivan-Mukta is he who has totally surrendered himself to God; so much so, that God alone works through him, his individual ego having been conquered. He always lives in God and God lives in him. He craves for no fame, no wealth, no earthly pleasures of any kind. In the inner consciousness of his being he finds the source of all bliss, and so lives contented under all conditions; no change of any kind in his life disturbs the even tenor of his mind.

He remains under all conditions at peace with himself. Nothing daunts him.

If he undertakes any work, it is always without any selfish motive; and no threat or pain or even death will prevent him from the performance of such work, since he takes it that the work is enjoined on Him by God Himself.

He may often have not even the feeling that God is working through him but he does all work without the least sense of egoism.

People in general will extol him at one time, and speak ill of him at another. He is bound by nobody's opinion.

He is free—ever free. Om Sri Ram!

The Pathless Path, p. 32

Self-Sacrifice: The Elimination of the Self

Self-sacrifice is the offspring of a well-regulated and well-controlled mind. Verily, the joy of existence lies in a life permeated with the spirit of complete self-denial. A life which depends upon itself for its highest happiness freely flows in acts always conducive to the happiness of the world at large. A narrow, self-conceited and selfish life has stranded many a man on the rocks of fear, doubt and misery.

A candle burns and spends its substance away in giving more and more light. The flower goes on giving out its sweet fragrance until it fades away and dies. The fire emits heat to the fullest capacity until its last embers turn into ashes. So a soul garbed in the robes of Divine joy gives himself away in all his varied actions through the mind and body for the weal of the world until the body drops off. Hence self-sacrifice, i.e. the elimination of the self in all that he does, far from being a painful experience, assumes the form of a spontaneous flow of delight.

Many do not know that the secret of true joy lies in self-sacrifice and not in self-seeking. The more you expand yourself, the more you diffuse your individual sense and merge in the totality of all objects and things, the nearer you approach the root of immortal and self-existent bliss.

Hence our great saints and sages have glorified the greatness of renunciation. Verily, renunciation alone leads the struggling soul into the realm of absolute peace.

The Divine Life, p. 109

Selfishness is the Root of All Evil

When a man is free from the clutches of the ego and its desires, in whatever field of activity he may be engaged, Karma cannot bind him.

The ego-sense is individual consciousness, in which a man thinks that he is a mere body, formed out of the five elements, and that he is the doer, as a separate Jiva.

To be engaged in the activities of Prakriti and still enjoy the bliss of the Atman, is possible when the idea of "I and mine" has been totally given up.

The only thing that a man has to renounce in order to attain the supreme Truth is the individual sense and nothing else.

The ego is an obsession, a shadow, an illusion; all life is one, and that one is yourself.

That the ego-sense is the cause of man's fall from his supreme state of blessedness and peace is evident in this wonderful Lila of the Lord.

To be conscious always that our individual life is only a thing of play, while in reality we are the ever free, all-blissful and omnipresent Spirit or Truth, is to be free from egoism

Do not forget the truth that nothing here belongs to you. All, including yourself, belong to the supreme Lord of the universe. The sense of possession is one of the main characteristics of the ego-sense.

The individual struggle, started and continued from the egoistic standpoint, in which God had no part to play, reveals only the weakness and helplessness of the aspirant.

Give up the individual "I". God only is, and He is all. Even your Sadhanas are not yours. Whatever you do is His act, It is He, within and without and everywhere. He is at once the actor and the non-actor. He is all.

The ego or the sense of separation is false. There is only one limitless ocean of joy, at once moving and still. There is one light, one power, one consciousness, one existence, one sole Reality, that is eternal and infinite.

Your life and all its activities belong to God. Do not undertake to follow any course prompted by the ego-ridden mind.

Truly, selfishness is the root of all evil. You see it magnified in others when you yourself have it in full.

To rise above the ego-sense, the path of devotion to the supreme Lord of the universe is the only way.

We can be good, and can do good, only when we act and live in the exalted state which is bereft of the egoistic notion of actorship. Real good flows out of us, only when we have transcended the individual sense and have come to dwell in the supreme and universal consciousness of God.

No change of situation can bring us peace and rest until the ego-sense of actorship is swept away. When we have realised that God's will alone works in all beings, and that the individual onus of action is false, external circumstances and situations cannot affect us.

The Sayings of Ramdas, pp. 3-5

Service is Work Done Out of Pure Love

Life fulfils its supreme purpose when it is imbued with the spirit of service. Service is the very perfume of a true life of love and sacrifice. Labour is the natural form of life, because life itself is activity, but when labour is inspired by love, it assumes the name of service. Service for gain, service for reward are the terms commonly employed. Here the significance of service loses its true colour and glory. Real service is work done out of pure love and compassion. Service thus rendered liberates life and fills it with the joy of the Eternal. The expression: "Do all your actions in the name of and for the sake of God" connotes that your life's activities be performed as pure offerings of love and for the fulfilment of love, because love is God and God is love.

The mother toils in the service of her child through selfless love for the sheer joy of the service. This service demands no return, is content in itself and is, therefore, ever permeated with the highest delight of life. When this very spirit of love, that actuates the mother to the careful and unstinted service of her child, enters into the entire movements and actions of life in its dealings with the life of the world, it becomes a veritable embodiment of free, universal and blissful service. Here the pains of service and sacrifice are not only bravely endured, but are also transmuted into pure emotions of joy.

O the glory of human life! How blissfully can it be converted into the Divine, if it is dedicated to the service of God in all beings and creatures of the world! One Truth, One Life, is the fact about the universe and everything in it. To tune human life to the knowledge of this Truth is the secret of the unfettered and free flow of it along the channels of Divine love and service.

The Divine Life, pp. 108-109

Silence is Brahman

My Beloved said in unmistakable words, "Until you transcend the relative, phenomenal life and know you are the absolute Truth, there is no liberation for you from the thraldom of fear and death, sorrow and pain, doubt and hate. Rise, rise, my child, from all dualities and dwell in the immutable, infinite Truth and Existence."

The multicoloured flowers and the green and yellow leaves, the zigzag creepers and grown up trees, the bare twigs and emerald fruits; the bright skies, the slow moving breezes; the play of bonny children are all so many dazzling pictures, displaying Thy magnificent glory, my Beloved.

I sit silent, wonder-struck, as it were, at seeing myself everywhere. It is silence in the depths of my being, pervading also my manifest life. Verily, silence is Brahman. It alone exists. Sounds are modulations of silence. Similarly, forms are expressions of the Formless. Truth or God alone is.

When the great day of illumination dawned, the worlds seemed to me as so many radiant bulbs suspended in the universe—a pageant of scintillating meteoric lights, engulfing all things in a mass of splendour in which this galaxy of orbs appears and disappears. The soul is then bathed in peace ineffable. I am that peace.

My Beloved comes to me in various shapes and forms. Human beings seek me from far and near in order to behold their real Self in me. What delight and joy they get! They cling on to me as long as they can and then away they go. Wherever they go, there is that Self. Self-vision is God-vision.

I am enthroned in the hearts of all beings and things. All beings and things are enthroned in my heart. Truly, their hearts and my heart are one. What a wonderful identity! I—the cosmic I—alone am. If there are two, I am that two too.

I sought Him. I found Him as myself. My voice rang forth a call for Him. I myself gave the response. I gazed everywhere and saw myself. I give and talk to myself, love and serve myself; for, there is none but I. My inward being is as clear as crystal. My vision is pure and stainless. My life flows like a sparkling stream with blissful spontaneity.

The Divine Life, pp. 61-62

The Soul Experiences a New Birth

There is a stage in the evolution of the soul when it takes an upward turn and rapidly marches towards the fullness and perfection of its inherent state of divinity. The soul is essentially divine, and to realise this it should, by a conscious process, return to its native spiritual greatness and glory. When this transformation takes place, the soul experiences a new birth, as it were, since it is imbued with a consciousness whose nature is eternal and infinite. It dawns on the soul that it is not a relative, limited and changing individual but that it is an omnipresent, imperishable and immutable Reality.

Now the soul undergoes such a change in its outlook that its valuation of life and its objects become entirely different from what it was before the spiritual enlightenment. Its life thereafter is lived in the terms of the absolute and all its activities are based upon the highest spiritual knowledge and experience.

Such a new birth and consciousness come to every soul in the world. Some may attain this blessed state earlier than others, but all human beings are inevitably progressing towards this ultimate, sublime consummation in their life-journey through the field of time and space.

The spiritual awakening of the soul is nothing but God revealing Himself in the heart. It is His omnipotent will prevailing over His lower nature behind the mask of which the supreme grandeur of the Divine is hidden. It is by a double process that the soul realises its spiritual sovereignty—God's assertion from within and the vehicle's submission to Him from without. The dominance of the former brings about the complete surrender of the physical, mental and vital aspects. It is like a brilliant light newly lit within a perforated screen permitting its radiance to spread out in all directions, converting even the screen itself into a mass of splendour.

The great Ones, who have reached the summit of divine illumination and knowledge, can alone lead and guide the souls that are struggling on the Path. It is by their power and grace that the aspiring soul is gifted with strength, courage and determination to boldly face all trials and surmount all obstacles on its way to the supreme goal. They inspire by contact, by teaching and by their power. They are like the gardeners who tenderly watch, nourish and take care, in every way, of the growing plant and see that it fulfils its existence by bearing beautiful flower and delicious fruit.

So, to quicken the soul with the longing for the Divine and to cause it to evolve steadily until it realises the fullness of its spiritual glory, the goodwill and blessings of a saint are absolutely necessary. The soul, caught in the toils of its lower nature, hungers for true freedom and happiness. This quest can easily, and in the shortest time possible, be fulfilled when it draws light, inspiration and grace from a saint. Truly, saints are saviours. They are the storehouses of spiritual wealth and they freely give it to those who ask them. To serve them is to have the right and the power to enter into the realm of immortality. All those who keenly desire for the spiritual unfoldment of their lives and the achievement of true happiness and peace should, in all meekness, approach saints and get illumined in their elevating and transmuting presence.

Now the new birth, the new life and the new consciousness will come to you as God's spontaneous gift and your life will be flooded with divinity inside and out. You are all the sacred and holy temples of God. May He manifest Himself in you and may you by His benediction become His incarnate images!

The Divine Life, pp. 29-30

Spirit and Matter are One and the Same

Truth pervades everywhere and that is my Beloved. Life enlivens all beings and things, and that is my Beloved. Joy eternal throbs in the hearts of all objects, and that is my Beloved. Light enlightens the entire universe, and that is my Beloved. Power activates all nature, and that is my Beloved. Peace perennial informs and animates whatever is visible and perceived, and that is my Beloved. O ever existent Truth! How can I envisage and describe Thee!

I am the witness of my silence and of my talk. I am silence and I am talk. What a wonder! Can I say this is mystic experience? It is more deep and more comprehensive than mysticism. What is it then? It is an inexpressible secret.

God and Soul: God is Soul. Soul is God. The vestures of the Soul—all bodies and forms are also God. Essentially, Spirit and matter are one and the same. Spirit in movement is energy. Energy condensed is matter.

There is no inner and outer existence. Divine existence is all in all. In all aspects and concepts It alone is. It, She or He—all is my Beloved—the Truth, God. God is form and also formless. I endeavoured to know Him and became He. Every thought and feeling of mine is inspired with this experience—I am He.

Life is space. Life is time. Life is causeless cause. Space is infinite. Time is eternal. God is life—infinite and eternal. Space encompasses all things. Time engulfs all things. I am such a God, such a life—spaceless, timeless and causeless. This is imagination run riot. It is a mad attempt to find out what I am, what God is.

When I talk I am dumb. When I walk I am still. When I work I am at rest. I do nothing when I move the worlds. All dynamics are mine, while I am the static Truth. Verily, I am and I am not. Can I apply this to my God? I am none else but He.

God is presence. God is absence. He is remembrance. He is obliviousness. He is myself. He is yourself. When I look at Him I see myself. I have His vision when I appear before myself. I realise Him when I know myself. How are we mixed up: He and I! Why not conclude, I and He are one.

The Divine Life, pp. 211-212

Spiritual Freedom Should be the Goal of Life

The charm and glory of life manifest when it is tuned with and merged in the great Universal Self who pervades all forms, objects and things. The soul which is imprisoned within the toils of individualism now attains the bliss of perfect freedom. Either on the physical plane or on the spiritual, man's hunger is for freedom. True freedom means real peace and happiness. The spiritual freedom is distinctly superior to the mere physical freedom; because whilst the latter grants man merely a touch of happiness, the former yields everlasting blisss. A man spiritually liberated, though physically bound, has realised eternal happiness, but not the man who is spiritually bound though physically free.

Hence spiritual freedom should be the goal of life if a soul would aspire to enjoy eternal felicity. The soul must lose itself in the infinite Spirit. In such an absorption, the soul identifies itself with that supreme Spirit. In any state, however exalted, in which the identification with the great spirit is not attained, perfect liberation and pure, everlasting joy are never possible. The absolute, the immortal, the great Reality is ever one. Any existence conceived of as secondary, equal or different from it can only be relative and hence not perfect. The wave and the ocean, the light and the sun are in their essence one and the same, although to the clouded vision they appear to be different. So in the absolute essence of Reality, God, Universe and the individual soul are one.

The upward flight of the soul is always towards this perfect identity with the great One who is the same through and in all. The river of life struggles through all obstacles and conditions to reach the vast and infinite ocean of existence—God. It knows no rest, no freedom and no peace until it mingles with the waters of immortality and delights in the vision of infinity.

The Divine Life, pp. 39-40

Spiritual Practice: Some Simple Rules

Invite God who is all Love and Mercy to take you up and transform you into His radiant and blissful child. Permit His Grace to purify, vitalise and take possession of every part of your being. Surrender your all to Him and be conscious of His presence within you and without you.

Meditation at stated times and remembrance of God at all times is necessary in the case of all Sadhakas. Conceive a thirst and hunger for God. Feel discontented for want of that hunger. A lukewarm desire does not result in much progress. Pray to God to give you that keen hunger. If you do Sadhana, you will get that hunger. Only be thorough and steady. Do not do things off and on. Have your Sadhana every day with greater and greater intensity.

While in the period of Sadhana, never bother yourself with the thought of Siddhis. Realise God first, and all else will come to you automatically. All doubts depart as Sadhana becomes regular.

The path of the spiritual aspirant is not an easy one; but one who is determined to progress along it, is sure to reach the goal.

The only way to control the mind and free it from undesirable thoughts is to put your life under strict discipline. Above all, don't come under the insinuating influence of laziness and inactivity. There is no greater enemy that comes in the way of an aspirant's advance on the path than laziness.

The simple rules are as follows:

1. Get up in the morning not later than five o'clock. Utilise the morning hour till six o'clock in the repetition of the Divine Name and meditation of the Lord's exalted attributes.

2. Take only Satwic, i.e., non-irritant food and eschew all stimulants.

3. Don't read flimsy and sensational literature but be reading the lives of saints and their teachings.

4. Never enter into discussion on religious or any other subjects with anybody.

5. Be unassuming and simple in your habits of life.

6. Be good, kind and serviceable to all who are in need of sympathy and assistance.

7. Keep the Name of God always on your lips whenever you are disengaged from other works.

8. Conceive a love for solitude and have resort to it now and again so that you can more easily tune your thought with God in an undisturbed place.

9. Seek the society of saints.

10. Maintain Brahmacharya.

11. Don't court the society of men who are immersed in sensual pleasures.

12. In other words, keep yourself perfectly pure in thought, word and deed.

A well-regulated life, having a keen sense of duty, and a patient and cheerful nature, are the characteristics of a true devotee of God.

Do not be impulsive and take steps to change the course of your present life and then give room for repentance. The goal is the awareness of your immortal existence and selfless service to humanity. You have to begin to work out this lofty object in the position in which you are at present. Of course there is struggle and difficulty. Nothing great can be achieved without a strenuous endeavour.

The easiest method for concentration is repetition of the Divine Mantram. Spend some time early morning and in the evening in the remembrance of God. Read *Bhagavad Gita* everyday. Lead a pure and simple life. Be kind and helpful to all who come in contact with you. Believe that the service of the suffering and the needy is the service of the Lord.

Never speak or encourage talk about yourself. Avoid all personal references. Speak always of Ram—His glories, His power and His peace.

Give up all externalities and show—even show of piety.

The Sadhaka should take very light food in the evenings. He must have only moderate sleep. He must never sleep in the afternoon or during the day. He must avoid worldly associations.

The true way is not an absolute seclusion for meditation, nor, a total absorption in the activities of life in pursuit of material ends, but a combination of the two, i.e., some hours of the day set apart for meditation so that the work in which we would be engaged during the other hours may be done as a spontaneous and blissful outflow of the Eternal Reality dwelling within us.

Do not engross yourself in action, however noble and beneficent, without knowing the Eternal Source of all action within you.

Question: *Which is the main pitfall a spiritual aspirant should be guarded against, when he is walking on the path of God-realisation?*

Answer: That is, spiritual pride due to a conceited consciousness of his progress on the path.

What often stands as an obstruction in the way of aspirants' attaining the goal is the ego-sense (vanity) born of a consciousness of his various acts of self-discipline. He thinks that he is superior to others because of the austerities he performed. Therefore it would be well for the Sadhaka from the very inception of his Sadhana to tutor the mind from time to time, into thinking that the works of Sadhana done by him are so done by the will and power of the Lord alone.

A Sadhaka should not reveal his spiritual experiences to anybody except to his Guru or a Saint. If he does not follow this rule, he will not only not receive a sympathetic hearing but also he will become so conscious of his spiritual advancement that this will prove a great impediment to his progress.

Whenever dejection overtakes the aspiring soul in his struggle, let him ward it off by surrender to the in-dwelling spirit.

Dive down deep within yourself and bring out the pearls of your own spiritual experience. Reveal your own light. Be the blazing Sun of Truth yourself and beautify your life and that of the world.

Imitation is dangerous. Each soul must seek his evolution on the spiritual path in his own individualistic and unique way.

To increase Bhakti, three things are necessary:

(i) Constant repetition of Ram-Nam;

(ii) To see Ram in all objects and beings;

(iii) To undergo all difficulties in a spirit of resignation and renunciation.

Steps that lead to surrender:

(i) Acknowledgement of God's will as supreme;

(ii) Realisation that God is always good and loving;

(iii) Acceptance of the fact that God has assumed the form of the Universe, of all creatures, of all beings and things in it.

There is no greater victory in the life of a human being than victory over the mind. He who has controlled the gusts of passion that arise within him and the violent actions that proceed therefrom is the real hero. All the disturbances in the physical plane are due to chaos and confusion existing in the mind. Therefore to conquer the mind through the awareness of the great Truth that pervades all existence is the key to real success and the consequent harmony and peace in the individual and in the world. Any amount of patch-work on the surface for the attainment of equilibrium and tranquillity can be of no avail. The heart should be purged of its base ambitions for material wealth, fame, possession and power at the expense of others.

The true soldier is he who fights not the external but the internal foes.

The Pathless Path, pp. 17-22

Sri Aurobindo

Question: *For the purpose of getting concentration, is it possible to combine the method of Japa which you teach and the method which Sri Aurobindo advocates?*

Ramdas: What is that method?

Question: *What I exactly mean is whether the object which can be attained by following your method and by Sri Aurobindo's method is the same.*

Ramdas: His method and Ramdas' method do not seem to be different because what he teaches is complete surrender to the Divine Power. Ramdas also teaches the same thing. By continuous remembrance of God, your ego-sense disappears and you surrender yourself to the Divine Will and Power by which you know that you as an individual are not doing anything by yourself, but a Divine Power that pervades the entire universe is responsible for all your activities—mental and physical. What Sri Aurobindo calls Shakti Upasana or worship of the Divine Power is the same as surrender to the Divine Will by continuous repetition of God's name. Repetition of God's name is a means employed for eradicating the ego-sense. When the mind continuously remembers God, ego-sense has no place in you. Your mind merges in a superconscious state and your actions then are not done by you, but by the Divine Power that is dwelling within you. This takes you to the sublime teaching of the *Bhagavad Gita*:

"Relinquishing all Dharmas take refuge in Me alone;
I will liberate thee from all sins; grieve not:"

This means that abandoning everything you must take Him as your supreme goal. God in you is making you do everything and you, as an individual doer, do not exist.

Question: *Sri Aurobindo teaches that self-surrender can be effected only gradually and I suppose that goes without saying. But there must be at the same time a decisive turn taking place in us. Should we think of that turn as something happening or should we simply concentrate on God and leave it to Him to do as He thinks best for us in His own time?*

Ramdas: What we have to do is to aspire for God. When this aspiration becomes intense, God helps in our progress and by His grace lifts us up and absorbs us into His all-inclusive, all transcendent Supreme Being.

Ramdas Speaks, vol. 2, pp. 125-126

Suffering and Sacrifice Soften the Heart of Man

The infinite power that controls the destinies of the universe and the countless worlds and creatures in it is a deep mystery. This great secret has baffled the intellect of the keenest thinker and eluded the cognisance of the greatest scientist. The laws that govern the universe do not seem to synchronise with even the most intelligent human conceptions of justice, law and order. To the bewildered man of the pragmatic mind, the workings of the universe appear to be arbitrary and chaotic. This is so because the practical man evaluates the changes and movements in the world-phenomena from his intensely individualistic and therefore circumscribed vision. Whenever a sudden change is observed in the workings of nature, affecting humanity, his first and only concern is to test how it touches him individually as a human unit. If he finds that the occurrence upsets the order of humanity, as conceived by him, he is disturbed and, more often than not, utterly confused. He questions, "Why is this and wherefore?" and comes to deny or doubt the existence of a guiding divine principle underlying all life and manifestation. He thinks that the universe is only a nightmare of wild and lunatic forces that clash and interclash without plan or purpose. He arrives at this conclusion, because he is groping only on the surface for solving the riddle of the universe. He does not probe deeper into the realm of the Spirit, for he would not believe in such a realm. This is so far as the rational man is concerned.

Now what does the man of intuition and inspiration, whose experience of the ultimate Reality that lies beneath the surface of things is as solid and actual as—nay, more solid and more real than—the experience of the man of intellect, declare? He definitely says that the universe is ever controlled by an invincible, inscrutable and omnipresent Divine power which is immortal, all-wise and all-blissful. To these sages the entire universe stands revealed as an open book. They behold it as nothing but an ordered and harmonious cosmos. They see before their universalised vision the unfoldment of grandiose, cosmic phenomena, evolved or projected forth from one eternal essence of Truth. As the single seed sprouts and grows into a variegated tree, so from the one immutable source has come forth the countless worlds and its creatures that make up the universe.

These sages, illumined with wisdom, proclaim that the worlds are God Himself in manifestation and the entire aspect of it His Lila or play. Creation, preservation and destruction constitute the movement of this play.

If the rationalist or the scientist, who relies solely on the conclusions of his intellectual and sense perception or on his observation and research, would only, with as much zeal and concentration as he employs in his quest for the secrets of mere external nature, attempt to dive into the depths of his being and discover the root power from which his intellect, sense and all movements of the physical nature derive their animation and energy, he could unfailingly solve the riddle that perplexes him.

What is the condition for this great vision and great attainment? A consciousness of unity with all life and all objects about us, far and near, is the condition. The separative vision of the soul must sublimate into the cosmic and all-pervading Spirit. The cramped understanding must expand and embrace infinity. The individual should be transformed into the universal.

At present we are face to face with the havoc brought about by the repeated and destructive shocks of earthquakes in Bihar, Orissa, Nepal and other surrounding provinces of Northern India. Difficult indeed for the rationalist to reconcile these workings of God with His attributes of love, mercy and peace. Still, the mystic sage maintains that it is all God's work and all for good. The path of salvation, i.e. the realisation of freedom lies through suffering and tribulation. The sufferer is blessed, and he who is touched by the woes of the sufferer and thus sacrifices his energy and wealth for his relief is also blessed. For, suffering and sacrifice soften the heart of man, and free it from pride, passion and ignorance, the essential thing needed for his liberation from the thraldom of the individual sense and its fetters.

In the absolute sense, God's acts pertaining to creation, preservation and destruction do not come under the classification of good and evil, yet in so far as His dispensations tend to revive the deadened human soul and awaken it to the consciousness of his inherent Divinity, God is indeed a most loving and benevolent parent of us all.

Therefore, the suffering that calls for and receives Divine assistance, and the sacrifice born of a compassionate heart, revealing in acts of succour, relief and service, gloriously mingle and realise the supreme unity in the infinity of Divine love and peace.

The Divine Life, pp. 350-352

Suffering is Essential for the Evolving Life

Adversity and misfortune and the resultant sorrow and suffering are the common lot of mankind. Some notable men of philosophic turn of mind have questioned the utility of suffering in the world, and have not only denied the goodness of God but have also flung Him out of human calculations as unworthy of belief. But men of true wisdom and perfected experience, who have probed deep into the mysteries of life, acclaim with no uncertain voice the invaluable uses of adversity. Surely, if there were no suffering in the world, there could be no evolution of man towards the highest destiny of life—the knowledge of immortality. It is through sorrow alone a soul understands the real foundation and purpose of existence. Misery, pain and suffering open the portals of his life to the comprehension of the supreme value and power of life. Progress towards the subtle and spiritual realms of existence is possible only along the path of pain and suffering. The fullest grandeur and beauty of life can be revealed when it is made to pass through the fire of tribulation and sorrow.

Every new birth presupposes a period of agony. Every seed breaks up with pain and manifests the charm of its hidden foliage and fruit. The innocent and smiling babe is revealed from behind the veil preceded by the mother's pains. The glowing stream of gold runs out of the dull ore when heated in the fiery furnace. The aroma of certain leaves and barks spreads out only when crushed and bruised. So also the life which is attended with the most painful experiences exhibits its highest glory.

Life would indeed be a stale and insipid thing if it were foreign to sorrow and pains. Because true beauty, power, peace and joy are born and nurtured in the womb of pain. The taste of sweetness is most enjoyed when it follows the taste of bitterness.

So do not depreciate the value of suffering. It is an element essential for the evolving life. Do not be afraid of suffering or attempt to run away from it. Realising its great need and use in the upward march of the soul to the goal of its immortal consciousness, welcome all the trials and struggles of life and derive therefrom increased powers of the will so that you can make the very sufferings as stepping stones to the heights of absolute peace and bliss. For the soul who has attained to the bliss and peace of immortality, suffering and pain are no longer suffering and pain. His entire life and all its experiences are transmuted into one ceaseless flow of ineffable ecstasy. Here sorrow and pain reach their supreme triumph. Those who have achieved this victory alone know the sweet uses of long suffering. It is they who proclaim that God, the creator of the worlds, is all goodness and benevolence. They do not find fault with the conditions existing in the world, because they know that the darkest moments of life herald the dawn of a radiant light of everlasting peace and happiness.

So glorify suffering and, understanding its true purpose in your life, make the right use of it. Instead of being cowed down by it, raise yourself and aspire for the higher and nobler aims of life. Cheerfully invite suffering, keeping in view the loftiest goal of life—the great Reality that lies at the basis of your and world existence. May the sublime possibilities of life be revealed in you by the transmuting touch of suffering. Let suffering cause to flower your soul so that it might emit the perfume of infinity, the bliss of eternity, and shine forth with that light, peace and love which is unconditioned and absolute. Blessed indeed are those that suffer.

The Divine Life, pp. 84-86

Surrender: The Most Natural and Easiest Path

The path of self-surrender is the most natural and the easiest path. Offer up everything to Ram. Lay your whole existence as a complete and unqualified offering at the holy feet of Ram. Behold the whole universe as the manifestation of Ram. Rejoice in seeing the worlds since they all remind you of Ram. Ram is light, love and bliss. You have nothing to condemn. The world is the Lila of Ram. Ram is playing in it by assuming various forms. Observe the play and remain always peaceful and full of bliss.

Offer up everything to Ram, your actions, words and thoughts, your body, mind and soul. Remember God at all times. He will then give you peace. Let all desires vanish in Ram. Let all the so-called evil disappear in Ram. Let all thoughts rest in Ram. Be absorbed and merged in Ram. Be mad with Ram. Be intoxicated with Ram. Then you have all that you have wanted. You have realised Ram, you have reached Truth, you have attained peace.

No bewilderment, no doubt, no struggle, when one has handed oneself completely into the hands of God. Live a life in complete submission to Ram, and you have no anxieties, no cares, no sorrows, no confusion. Do not mind what people say of you. Remain firm in your faith in Ram, in praise and ignominy alike. Do not condemn anything; seek no advice; don't be led away; exercise your own will, i.e., the will of Ram. Don't dwell upon personalities; all forms are unreal; all opinions are nothing to you; cling to Truth, Peace, Love, Light, Bliss. Have no misgivings. Be peaceful, contented and blissful. Ram is the only Reality. Meditate on Ram, always. See only Him everywhere. Ram, Ram. Om Sriram.

At the Feet of God, pp. 54-55

Surrender to God

The aim of all religions is to point out the path that leads to perfect freedom, peace and joy. This blessed state can be realised only by the eradication of the ego-sense through surrender to God.

Divine life should flow through us, divine love should dwell in our hearts, and divine light should inspire all our activities. Therefore our heart should be attuned to His love, our intellect be illumined with His wisdom and our body be worked at His will. This is the goal of human life.

To teach this great truth came Krishna, Buddha, Christ and Mohammed. They declare in one voice that we can reveal the hidden Divinity in us by resigning ourselves to Him totally and dedicating our life to His service.

Mere intellectual understanding of religious truths is different from actual spiritual experience which is a matter of intimate relationship between the soul and God.

It must be understood that to love and serve God is to love and serve all beings and creatures. To realise God is to be conscious of His presence everywhere. Wherever you turn, there is His light, power and glory.

Spiritual discipline which a man performs under the inspiration of the Divine can alone purify him and make him aware of the immortal Spirit which is God. All else is, as the saying goes, 'sheer vanity and vexation'.

Let us live and act as He wills for the universal good. Verily, to love and serve all constitutes true enlightenment, liberation and peace—this is the loftiest achievement.

The Divine Life, pp. 370-371

The Triune Path

Devotee: *Which of the paths is the best?*

Ramdas: Man has intellect, heart and body. He should use the intellect for Vichara, i.e., he should discriminate between the real and the unreal so as to give up attachment to the unreal or the perishable things of the world, and meditate on the Real. In the heart he should develop love and devotion for God. With the body he must perform selfless work. Unselfish work will purify his mind, help his meditation and increase his devotion to God.

All these three practices must go together. This is called the triune path. There are people who take to any one of these and leave the other two. This is not good. It will be like exercising one part of the body and developing that part only to the exclusion of the rest. That would result in asymmetrical growth.

Gospel of Swami Ramdas, p. 483

Truth is Eminently Beautiful

Truth is eminently beautiful. All the visible and invisible worlds are the expressions of the Truth; hence loveliness and joy are spread out everywhere. To divinise life is to beautify it.

Truth is not merely silence—a stillness unrelieved and monotonous. Truth is all-comprehensive. It is at once static and dynamic. To emphasise any one aspect of it and say that that is all, is not right. Truth's glory lies in its revelation; hence Truth is love and love is beauty. To realise Truth is to make life unfold its divine loveliness—infuse into every part of it the lustre of grace and excellence. Life now blossoms like a fragrant flower, shedding its sweetness all around. If not this, what is the attainment of Truth worth? Life must come into contact with Truth so intimately that it can fully manifest itself in all its grandeur and glory.

In the name of Truth, looking upon it as something far off from the ken of men, life should not be made to assume a plain, crude and uncouth face. If tenderness and forgiveness do not illumine life, if goodwill and sympathy do not inform it, if love does not inspire it, what would it avail if it has all knowledge and has gained strange powers? Let your life be a movement of love and beauty and thus be a blessing to all.

It is not philosophy, however high-sounding, that can really sweeten life. It is simple love and joy that elevates, ennobles and liberates it. Meekness and gentleness are the handmaids who wait upon Truth. Calculation, conceit and harshness do not belong to a life imbued with divine beauty.

The votary of Truth, though unassuming and egoless, towers above all those who are vain and presumptuous of their spirituality. His life flows with a sweet murmur, gladdening the heart of everyone who comes to him. His heart throbs with the purest emotion; his head radiates a divine halo; he acts and moves in perennial ecstasy.

Therefore, he who is like unto the child is the rightful heir to the kingdom of eternal beauty and joy. Be therefore cheerful, free, innocent and egoless like a child, if you really wish to comprehend Truth. Open up every nook and corner of your being and eject out all the low passions and conceits that clog the system, and permit the divine splendour and bliss to reveal in you, and transmute your entire being into the very image of Truth. Let divine beauty thrill your heart, flash on your mind and permeate your actions.

There is a rare beauty in sacrifice. Beauty does not consist in talking of the serene depths of your being while making life a distorted and repulsive picture. As you give yourself away selflessly, you unfold, through sheer joy, the beauty of the indwelling Truth. Life is granted for the fulfilment of this supreme aim. Self-delusion is not realisation of the Divine. It is cleverness, pride and self-centredness that mar the beauty of life.

Imitation has seized the seekers of Truth and it has retarded, if not cut off entirely, their growth and progress. Lisping in the words of great souls is not a sign of genuineness. Dive deep down within yourself and bring out the pearls of your own spiritual experience. Reveal your own light. Be the blazing sun of Truth yourself and beautify your life and that of the world.

The Divine Life, pp. 21-22

Unity of Mankind

Essentially, humanity is one. Under the influence of nescience we create a sense of diversity and see distinctions and differences among the members of the human race. We possess a natural affinity to each other. Everyone of us possesses the same power of thought, feeling and action. We are blessed with speech, which is a splendid means by which we can communicate with each other. So we should think, feel and act in a spirit of love and unity.

The life-principle that activates all beings is the same. We all breathe the same air, walk on the same earth, and are equally entitled to the enjoyment of the amenities which nature provides. The earth yields its rich gifts to all alike. The differences between man and man on the material plane are, in truth, unnatural and improper. For, the component parts and composition of human bodies and the qualities inherent in them are not diverse and conflicting. If we look with the pure vision that belongs to an enlightened mind, we do not see any clear-cut line of demarcation that isolates man from man, one set of people from another, or one nation from another. We are indeed parts of a stupendous whole. We are units that form the world-community or family. So we can live and act as members of a world-brotherhood or federation.

This is proved to be true so far as the physiological and material side of life is concerned. Now let us go deeper through matter into Spirit. At the basis of this vast material manifestation there is one supreme all-pervading Reality. When this Reality is known, we rise above the body-consciousness and realise the unity of all existence in the realm of the Spirit. Really the same Truth dwells in all, the Truth that permeates all lives, not merely human, but also the animal and vegetable life. Nay, the Truth pervades the entire universe, both animate and inanimate. For him who has transcended the relative planes of life, all invidious distinctions disappear like mist in the sun. His heart blossoms into love for the entire creation. There is the Vedantic saying, *Sarvam Khalvidam Brahma*—verily, everything here is Brahman or Truth. For him, then, all beings, creatures and things are the revelations of the immanent and transcendent Spirit.

Now we know for certain that both materially and spiritually all beings on the globe are fundamentally one. Let us, through the use of our reason and, going still deeper, through a soul-realisation, discover the fact that we are co-related to each other in blood, flesh and spirit, and belong to the one united world-manifestation of the Spirit.

Thus world-brotherhood, in which there is no difference of race, country, nationality, creed and colour, becomes a reality. It is not a state to be newly achieved, but a truth to be realised and experienced. The awakening within us should enable us to shake off the illusion that possesses us, distorting our vision and creating unnatural clashes, discords and wars.

The only way to solve the world-problem is to break down this subversive mentality by plunging within ourselves, through self-control and purification, and find the supreme and all-pervading Spirit of our real being. In the great Scripture, the *Bhagavad Gita*, Sri Krishna says, "I am the Sutratman—the immanent Spirit that, like the thread in a rosary, links everything together. I pervade all beings and things as the Atman or Spirit, just as a string passes through the beads in a rosary." All beings are, therefore, strung as it were on the same Truth or

Spirit that pervades everywhere. So, looking at humanity from the vision of this indwelling Spirit, we are all one. The thread is gold, the beads are also gold. So also the formless, unmanifest, omnipresent Divine is one, and the forms, lives and things which are expressions of this eternal Reality are also one. World-brotherhood, international federation, unity of mankind, which all mean one and the same, have to be realised by everyone of us. Then only we can truly love and help each other without any hatred or ill will in our attitude, without any taint of self-seeking in our conduct towards our fellow-beings. In this lies our salvation, the way to peace and harmony, the supreme destiny and happiness of the human race.

The Divine Life, pp. 307-309

Vegetarian Food Will be Helpful

Question: *What do you think about vegetarianism. It is useful for concentration, is it not? Are you a vegetarian?*

Ramdas: Yes, Ramdas is a vegetarian. But he does not condemn non-vegetarians, among whom also there are devotees. He only tells them that if they want to concentrate their mind on God, vegetarian food will be helpful. It is Sattwic food. If one uses onions, garlic or chillies, he will find great disturbance in the mind and it will become restless. Meat also should be totally eschewed as it is Rajasic in nature and irritates the mind and proves a hindrance on the spiritual path. If you want concentration and contemplation on God, it is better to use such food as will not create disturbance in the mind. Therefore, carefully selected food is considered most suitable for spiritual aspirants.

Ramdas Speaks, vol. 2, p. 100

Vision of Equality

The devotee, who has purified his mind through the constant remembrance of God and dedication of all his actions to him, attains the supreme knowledge of the Atman. This knowledge makes him realise his perfect identity and oneness with the all-pervading, changeless, formless and eternal existence of God. In this experience the devotee, losing entirely his separate individual sense, becomes merged in the attributeless and infinite Reality. He realises that all the phenomenal manifestations are strung, as it were, on the one omnipresent, invisible and immortal Truth. In the supreme harmony, unity and equality of this vision, all sense of diversity and differentiation is dissolved. This vision of perfect equality lifts the devotee from the meshes of Gunas and fixes him in the unaffected, ever pure and unchanging truth of his existence, beyond the touches of pleasure and pain. Now the devotee attains the supreme bliss and peace, born of the consciousness of immortality. He is no longer the bewildered creature in the grip of the lower human nature belonging to ignorance, but is a free and liberated soul, in all the glory of his divine nature formed of the light of knowledge.

Before the devotee rises to the height of complete realisation of God's all-inclusive and all-comprehensive being, he has to transcend the Gunas and abandon his egoistic personality by the attainment of this exalted knowledge of the Atman. Verily, the devotee has to be reborn in the consciousness of God before he could put on the illumined vesture of a Divine personality.

When the devotee through intense longing and aspiration contemplates upon the eternal Beloved, seated within his own heart and the hearts of all beings and creatures, by the very force of his devotion he gets absorbed in the immutable essence of God. The devotee is the arrow and Bhagavan is the mark. The arrow strikes the mark and melts in the mark to such a degree that the arrow is completely transformed into the mark itself. So also, the devotee having complete union and oneness with God becomes God Himself.

In this vision of equality, the devotee does not behold the differences which are seen and taken to be real by the soul obsessed by ignorance. He sees the same truth alike in all beings and creatures. The distinctions of caste, creed, colour and race have no longer any significance for him. He looks upon the learned Brahmin and the so-called untouchable with the same vision of equality. In short, his life will now be perfectly blessed, since he enjoys the bliss and peace of immortality based upon his experience of harmony, unity and peace in all the varied expressions of life and phenomena. This extremely purifying knowledge opens out the floodgates of the highest vision of God in the universe and beyond. It is now that he beholds the entire universe as the one variegated and dazzling image of his supreme Beloved.

The Divine Life, pp. 125-127

War: What are We to Make of It?

The supreme Divine Principle at the root of the universal manifestation is one. From this eternal Source have sprung all creatures, beings and things. Again from this Source alone have emanated the varied forces that produce kaleidoscopic changes in the phenomena of nature. The creative and destructive forces alike issue from this great Origin. In fact, they are the two aspects of the same power—seen from different angles. When we view nature and its workings from the vision of the underlying basic Reality, our conceptions of good and evil dwindle out. It is now that we behold the universe in all its colours, forms, transmutations, even amidst the clash and conflict of opposing forces, as utterly Divine. Because all these have come forth from one Eternal Principle, being the revealment of one immortal essence.

The question which is now looming prominently before us is: why should there be war in the world — war that ruthlessly brings about the destruction of human life on an extensive scale, involving the wanton slaughter of also the innocent and non-combatant peoples? Again, why should earthquakes, floods, famines and pestilences devastate the earth from time to time? The perplexed mind of man further asks: why God, who is held to be the very spirit of compassion, love and mercy should permit catastrophes to convulse humanity? We strenuously cudgel our brains to probe into the mysterious workings of God for a solution. But we are baffled and feel helpless, for however deeply we might think on these problems, the mind has no explanations to offer. It confesses its inability to throw light upon them inasmuch as it finds that its range and grasp are but narrow and limited. Even the very idea it forms of compassion and love seems to be too hazy, volatile and indecisive. So any attempt to solve this supreme question of questions intellectually leads us nowhere. Very often in such a case where does the struggle of the mind end? It not only abandons the riddle as beyond its power to solve, but thereafter dwells in a stupefied consciousness of uncertainty, doubt and despair.

Man is no doubt a thinker, but this thinking faculty is his weakness as much as it is his strength. Thought is capable of presenting us with only one aspect of the infinite Truth. In order to possess a comprehensive knowledge of the Truth we have to transcend thought. The right use we can make of the rare gift of reason is to rise above it.

Now what does the sage, who having transcended the intellect and attained to the wisdom of the eternal, say? He declares: I have discovered the great Cause—the very fountain-head—from which all the visible nature and the powers active in it issue forth. Reaching this Truth, I look on the world manifestation as it stands, without favour or prejudice. I clearly witness in all the transformations taking place before me, in the vast play of nature, the finger of one supreme Being—in the so-called good as well as the evil forces that cause the momentous revolutions in the destinies of the worlds and its beings. My optimistic vision, which beholds Divinity manifest everywhere, is never marred by even the greatest calamities and disasters that befall the earth and its creatures. God is manipulating the world for a rapidly progressive evolution, towards a higher order of things by means of cataclysmic upheavals in the affairs of men.

Let us face things in the world as they are. Creation and destruction are twin forces that work concomitantly for the control and adjustment of the universe. The world is by nature the play of these opposing forces. You cannot imagine a particular mode of movement alone to prevail at all times. Since every move runs along a circle, there is no such thing as an absolutely straight course in the dynamics of progression. The opposites meet and extremes coalesce. The world of nature is there before us as the combined expression of these conflicting forces which are ever engaged in a hand to hand tussle for overcoming each other. So we have to take the world as it is. It cannot be otherwise than what its innate tendencies and qualities could make it. Stand apart in the stillness and silence of your undying and unchanging Spirit, and play the part which the Divine power active in you and the world has appointed for you. The power in the manifestation and the unaffected immutable Spirit behind it are one in the all-inclusive and all-transcendent Truth. Know this and be free from the bondage of death, fear and sorrow.

To revert to our question: what are we to make of war? In what manner could it prove to be of spiritual value and make for the regeneration of humanity? It is to be admitted that war opens out avenues for the expression of the noblest virtues and traits inherent in the human being. The highest types of the developed human life are the outcome of the crucial and fiery ordeals through which it is made to pass. Under these conditions alone we observe that the intellect and the heart are pitched to the summit of their evolution.

The lustrous glory of the day is there because of its juxtaposition with the gloomy darkness of the night. The death-dealing din of battle has produced heroes of supernatural valour. The agony of war has given birth to rare angelic souls who wore their lives out, ministering to the disabled, wounded and sick. The levelling hammer of war has brought down proud and insolent authority to the dust. The cries and wails of war have softened the flinty hearts of millions who were steeped in selfish pleasures, purchased from exploited wealth. The universal impact of war has broadened the vision of mankind and also awakened in them a spirit of sympathy and love that radiates towards all beings on the globe.

It is war that produced the Gita—a scripture that leads the entrapped soul to the realm of immortality, freedom and peace. It is the cult of hate and murder that brought out in all its unique glory the Divine compassion and mercy of Christ on the Cross. In the battlefields of Arabia rose the Prophet Mohammed. An age of exploitation, cruelty and hypocrisy ushered into the world the great Buddha. Rama shone out as the glorious saviour when he achieved triumph in the conflict with the deadly forces of the demon Ravana. Prahlad, the ideal devotee, was a radiant child sprung from the wrath and ferocity of his tyrant father. From the mire of undeserved tribulation, destitution and suffering came forth the fairest flower of truth—Harischandra. Such instances can be multiplied.

Verily, "out of evil cometh good"—nay, evil itself is good, when we perceive that in its womb is nurtured the seed of good. Evil and good have no distinctive marks that distinguish them. It is our labelling them according to the dictates of a narrow vision or individualistic outlook which is the cause of all mischief. Evil is no evil when it is a precursor of good. In fact the so-called evil of every kind that affects human beings is God-ordained, as it is a necessary factor for the soul's march towards its ultimate destiny. Evil can never be counted as evil the moment we discover its right place and use as a vitalising element of life. Hence, war, earthquakes, pestilences, floods and such visitations on the earth have their supreme value and significance. They are really Divine acts of mercy, love and compassion. God's law always works for progress, and progress involves construction as well as destruction in the physical nature. Death is not the end of things. Death can be spoken only of the body. The soul is eternal, undying and indestructible. Every death wrung out by the fire of a lofty ideal liberates the soul into the knowledge of its immortality—a kingdom of absolute peace and bliss.

The absolute is alone good. It is a good above all mental standards, and this good or God is at the inception, along the evolution and in the ultimate absorption of all visible objects and things. He is the one power that creates and destroys—be it men or other creatures, be it on a smaller or a vaster scale. Man can be at peace with God and the world only when he looks upon all things and events as ever bearing the stamp of supreme goodness. The soul's ultimate state of beatitude, freedom and bliss is in this comprehensive knowledge of God and nature and its workings.

The Divine Life, pp. 346-350

Work is Worship When It is Done Selflessly

Ramdas does not want anyone to lead only a contemplative life. One must also serve one's fellow beings in a selfless spirit. "Love thy neighbour as thyself" does not mean that love should only be felt in the heart. It must be shown also in action, in the form of relieving distress and rendering help in all possible ways. To serve man is to serve God. In *Karma Yoga*, work is done as worship. Then alone it gives joy. It should be done as perfectly as possible, with great care and love and never in a slipshod, clumsy, irregular or half-hearted way. The inner beauty must reveal itself in outer conduct.

Do not renounce work but divinise work by doing it in full submission to the will of God. Work is worship when it is done selflessly in a spirit of dedication to God. Do not run away from the work given to you by the Divine. Do it without the ego-sense. Become willing instruments in the hands of the Divine and cheerfully do the work, without any thought of the fruits. Work, and be a detached witness of the work.

Thus Speaks Ramdas, paras 38-39

Yoga: Perfect Union with God

Yoga is the path by traversing which the individual soul realises its real nature of immortality, omnipresence, peace and bliss. The essential condition for the attainment of this supreme goal is the complete absence of the ego-sense. Self-control and self-discipline are the means. Yoga also signifies union with and absorption in the immortal Reality. A steady, persevering and concentrated effort and struggle alone can lead the aspirant to the realisation of the Godhead. So long as man is hankering after the pleasures of the senses, his progress on the path is slow and erratic. He must be undaunted in his endeavour and determined in his purpose. He must leave no stone unturned to subdue and eventually eradicate the impure passions of his heart and mind. A purified and enlightened Buddhi can alone entitle the Sadhaka to enter the kingdom of eternity.

Yoga is not a thing to be merely talked about, read in books and heard through others. Yoga is for practice in life. Yoga which does not soften the heart and fill it with the pure emotion of love, compassion and peace is not worth the name. Real concentration of mind and meditation of God in the chamber of his heart does bring about an enormous change in the devotee. His transformed life becomes a beacon light for others. Through thought, word and deed he pours out love and bliss upon all. If not to live such a life, what use is there for a man to speak of and wish to hear of Yoga?

Yoga is usually understood to mean the performance of some mysterious practices by which one becomes gifted with miraculous powers. And there are many who are keen upon the knowledge of this practice in order to gain these powers. A real Yogi does possess supernatural powers which he brings into play, if at all he makes use of them, for the uplift of humanity. These powers come to him in the usual course, he never works for them. If he does, the fullness of joy and ecstasy of his immortal Self and a continued flow of his heart in floods of love for all in the world would have no place in his life. Therefore the sole aim with which a devotee or a Sadhaka starts on the career of Yoga is only to attain perfect union with his God or complete liberation.

The Divine Life, pp. 112-113

Zoroaster Taught the Suzerainty of God

Sri Krishna declares in the *Gita* that whenever wickedness and unrighteousness prevail in the life of humanity, then the great Cosmic Spirit who rules over the affairs of the world, manifests Himself in order to destroy evil and establish peace, goodness and harmony. If we examine the periods, when the mighty Prophets and Avatars appeared, we discover that they came at such critical times of degeneration and discord. Zoroaster, the Prophet of Persia, incarnated in the country under similar conditions.

From the precious records of Zoroaster's teachings we see, that in fundamentals, his message from the Divine is perfectly in consonance with the messages of the Prophets of other climes and ages. The mission of a Prophet or Avatar is to awaken mankind to the knowledge of God and lead it on the path of purity and righteousness. Man can live in peace with man and enjoy the blessing of true happiness only when he rises above the warring passions of his heart and finds his abode in the infinite being of God. Zoroaster reveals in his teachings wherein lie the evils in human nature that keep man down and how, by eradicating them, he can be set free to soar up and be absorbed in the self-existent Divinity.

He held faith, prayer and a maintenance of strict discipline in individual and social life are the means to attain the exalted state. Here are some teachings culled from "Zend-Avesta":

Prayer to Thee, O Ahura-Mazda, is the giver of excellence, holiness, success and high exaltation—it is the act of virtue.

When my eyes beheld Thee, the essence of Truth, the Creator of life, who manifests his life in his works, then I knew Thee to be primeval spirit, Thou Mazda, so high in mind as to create the world, and the father of the good mind.

A virtuous man's soul is pure, and with the purity of the soul he can be possessed of the wisdom of the invisible world.

Take less care of your body and more of your soul.

Contentment is the happiest condition of man and the most pleasing to the Creator.

It is fruitless to expect to go to Heaven without a steadfast faith in God.

The man who is pious and good in every respect, is blessed with mental ease and happiness in this material world, and also exalted in the invisible or spiritual world.

Thus the Prophet—Zoroaster is a Teacher imbued with Divine light and inspiration. He taught the suzerainty of God above everything else. May his compassionate Spirit enliven the heart of man and engender in it true peace and harmony, born of the union and oneness with the Almighty Controller of the worlds.

The Divine Life, pp. 179-181

Bibliography

Fortunately the message of Swami Ramdas is being widely spread via his books. His works have been published not only in Western languages such as English, Italian and French but also in Indian languages such as Kannada, Malayalam, Telugu, Tamil, Hindi, Gujarati, Marathi, Sindhi and Bengali.

Arranged chronologically according to the dates when they were first published, all the books listed below are in English. Each of these items was published by Anandashram, P.O. Anandashram 671531, Kanhangad, District Kasaragod, Kerala, India.

WORKS BY SWAMI RAMDAS

In Quest of God (1925). This book vividly describes the experiences of Ramdas during the first year of his travels throughout India as a wandering monk, culminating in his spiritual Liberation.

At the Feet of God (1928). This book consists of the inspired utterances of Ramdas during the early years of his travels as a God-mad monk who saw Ram in everyone and everything. In her *Preface* Elizabeth Sharpe remarks: "Ramdas has found that happiness; that intense, never-fading joy; that perfect bliss which comes from God-realisation."

Gita-Sandesh (Message of the Gita) (1933). "The *Bhagvad Gita* holds forth before mankind the highest and the loftiest ideal by attaining which the soul is liberated from all limitations and enjoys the peace and bliss of his inherent state of immortality." With these words Ramdas commences his commentary on the *Gita*. The different kinds of Yoga are discussed and difficult points are elucidated.

Krishnabai (1933). "This beautiful though short sketch from the worthy pen of the Swamiji records the life of a seraphic soul who combines at once the divinity of the Mother with that of a radiant child of God, pure, innocent and ever blissful." (an excerpt from the *Foreword* by Rama Bai C.T.)

The Sayings of Ramdas (1933). This book was compiled by Dr. M.K. Shukla from the early letters of Ramdas to various devotees. It is replete with spiritual instructions, such as "A cheerful mind cures and wards off all mental and physical diseases."

The Vision. In October 1933 Ramdas began an international monthly entitled *The Vision*, which is dedicated to universal love and service. He personally edited this periodical during the first two years of its existence. Now in its 66th year of publication, this magazine consists mainly of interesting excerpts from the works of Ramdas.

The Divine Life (1934). This large collection of essays on various spiritual subjects contains the essence of Ramdas' teachings. His insights gained from Self-realisation stimulate readers to lead divine lives themselves.

In the Vision of God: Experiences in continuation of "In Quest of God" (1935). Whereas *In Quest of God* (1925) covered only one year of Ramdas' experiences as an itinerant religious mendicant, *In the Vision of God* is a narration of his later experiences during the subsequent nine years, until the founding of Anandashram in 1931. This latter book supplements the former one.

Letters of Swami Ramdas, 2 volumes (1940). Words of loving concern and advice to spiritual aspirants are aplenty in these letters which were written during the period 1928-32.

Poems (1940). His mystical emotions have been expressed in simple and rapturous words. Born of his direct experience of the Absolute, these poems are ecstatic and intensely devotional in nature.

Glimpses of Divine Vision (1944). A devotee by the name of T. Bhavani Shanker Rau selected these significant passages from the unpublished letters of Ramdas for the years 1933-35 and arranged them under appropriate headings, such as Sorrow and Pain, Faith, Peace and Meditation.

The Pathless Path (1947). Formerly published as *Guide to Aspirants,* this book is a very useful collection of quotations from Ramdas' works. "Gurudas", the compiler of this book, states that "These extracts represent the several rungs of the ladder of spiritual evolution."

Ramdas Speaks, 5 volumes (1955). These books of inestimable value, which cover Ramdas' talks and discourses during his 1954 world tour, were painstakingly and faithfully recorded by Swami Satchidananda.

World is God (1955). Ramdas has carefully chronicled his impressions of his 1954 world tour. He has described the remarkable people he met and the interesting places he visited.

Call of the Devotee (in continuation of *"In the Vision of God")* (1959). In response to the invitations of several devotees, Ramdas travelled in different parts of India during 1936-38 and 1949. All his spiritual instructions to various questioners are of perennial interest and some of the happenings he reports are full of humour.

Hints to Aspirants (1959). This book is a collection of excerpts from Ramdas' letters to his devotees the world over. His words are a great encouragement to all who are seeking after the Divine.

Ramdas' Talks (1959). This work was published for Anandashram by Bharatiya Vidya Bhavan. It contains selections from Ramdas' talks during his Indian tours in 1951-52.

Stories as Told by Ramdas (1959). Ramdas' *Foreword* states: "The book contains 108 stories. Many of the stories were either heard or read by Ramdas on various occasions. The reader will find in the book also stories told by Sri Ramakrishna, Sri Ramana Maharshi and other saints of India and abroad. The collection is by no means exhaustive. But the stories presented here will no doubt prove to be a source of instruction and enlightenment to the spiritual aspirant."

Thus Speaks Ramdas (1961). This pocket-book of quotations from Ramdas is a representative selection of his teachings.

God-Experience, 2 volumes (1963). Based on notes lovingly made by Swami Krishnananda Das, these 2 volumes cover the talks of Ramdas at Anandashram during the last years before his passing away in 1963. There is a wealth of information and advice on spiritual matters.

Swami Ramdas on Himself (1994). Ramdas shows how unswerving devotion and joyous resignation to the Divine Will led him to the summit of spiritual experience. These works were first published as "Papa on Himself" in *The Vision* during the years 1971-74.

WORKS ABOUT SWAMI RAMDAS

CHANDRA SHEKHAR

Passage to Divinity: The Early Life of Swami Ramdas (1946). This fascinating biography extends from Ramdas' birth to his renunciation of the world. This book incorporates *The Early Life* which is an autobiographical essay by Ramdas.

MOTHER KRISHNABAI

Guru's Grace (Autobiography of Mother Krishnabai) (1964).

Mother Krishnabai has described her years of struggle and how her meeting with Ramdas hastened her realisation of the Supreme. This intensely devotional book is addressed entirely to "Papa" (Ramdas) and all the persons mentioned therein are regarded by her as Papa himself in those forms. It was Ramdas who translated this work into English.

SWAMI SATCHIDANANDA
The Gospel of Swami Ramdas (1980). Some of the conversations of Ramdas and Mother Krishnabai, including anecdotes about them, have been faithfully recorded in this large book which is readable and profound at the same time.

SWAMI SATCHIDANANDA
Vishwamata Krishnabai (Some Glimpses) (1991). Swami Satchidananda's impressions of Mother Krishnabai, Ramdas' foremost disciple, are based on four decades of close association with her. He highlights her strong points and saintliness.

U.S. RAMACHANDRAN
Swami Satchidananda (A Thumbnail Sketch) (1991). Swami Satchidananda, who is today the guiding spirit of Anandashram, is the only disciple whom Ramdas initiated into Sannyas. The book describes his spiritual quest. Since 1947 he has been dedicated to serving Ramdas and his mission.